THE IMPOSTOR SYNDROME

HOW TO REPLACE SELF-DOUBT WITH SELF-CONFIDENCE AND TRAIN YOUR BRAIN FOR SUCCESS

THE IMPOSTOR SYNDROME

HOW TO REPLACE SELF-DOUBT WITH SELF-CONFIDENCE AND TRAIN YOUR BRAIN FOR SUCCESS

JOHN GRADEN

Big Dream Media, LLC

49108

CONTENTS

Endorsements for John Graden's, The Impostor Syndrome: How to Replace Self-Doubt with Self-Confidence and Train Your Brain for Success

"Your ability to realize your full potential requires that you release your 'mental brakes.' John Graden's excellent book, The Impostor Syndrome *shows you how to eliminate self-sabotage on the road to success."*

—Brian Tracy—Author
"The Way to Wealth"

The Impostor Syndrome *is a fascinating book that is easy to read with some very good advice for living a more fulfilling life.*

—Joe Hyams, Bestselling author of Bogie:
The Biography of Humphrey Bogart

"The Impostor Syndrome *is an invaluable book that every friend, employer, teacher, and leader will want to provide for the people in their lives. This is an issue that is seldom recognized or discussed, yet it holds so many back from reaching their potential."*

—Scott Kelby, Bestselling
Author with over one millions books sold

"90% of winning is mental and John Graden knows how to win. In his excellent book, The Impostor Syndrome, *John Graden lays out a step-by-step process for overcoming self-doubt and developing a champion's mindset. He is living proof what he teaches works. This gets my highest recommendation."*

—Tokey Hill
1999 Olympic Coach of the Year

"In order to become a psychologist, I wrote my thesis on The Impostor Syndrome *in adolescents. After reading John Graden's book,* The Impostor Syndrome, *I knew I was dealing with a master on this topic: this is a fantastic concept. The book teaches you how to program your mind to succeed and how to overcome the negative self-destructive tendencies we all suffer from. This book is extremely powerful and it will change your life forever."*

—Dr. Carmen Harra,
author of Everyday Karma

"John Graden's Impostor Syndrome *will free you from being paralyzed by self-doubt as he gives you permission to fake it until you make it. His book will also give you permission to live life far beyond your comfort zone and receive your own success without apologizing for it."*

—Dr. Lara Honos-Webb, author of The Gift of
ADHD and Listening to Depression, visionarysoul.com

"I am recommending your book, The Impostor Syndrome *to my clients because it will validate what I've always emphasized . . . . We can afford anything in life except being around negative thoughts and individuals—negativity is a self-propelling contagious disease that spreads like a raging fire on a path of self-destruction."*

—Dr. Gloria Gilbere

"The fear of failure is a common feeling among most people striving for success in business and life. The Impostor Syndrome, *by John Graden examines the causes for this inhibiting self-doubt and inspires readers with his empowering, proven strategies to overcome it."*

—Dr. Ivan Misner
NY Times bestselling author and Founder of BNI

"The Impostor Syndrome *is a welcome addition to the toolkit of anyone looking to break free from self-defeating habits and make real changes in the quality of his or her life. John Graden has spent his career helping others reach their physical, mental, and financial potential, and in the pages of this book, he offers his valuable insights and experience to a wider audience."*

—Scott Ries, LISW
Department of Psychiatry
University of Cincinnati

"A powerful guide for illuminating and breaking through your mental barriers and reprogramming yourself for lasting success and fulfillment. I love every morsel of what I read. Very powerful"

—Jill Koenig GoalGuru.com

"In over 20-years of photographing some of Hollywoods' biggest stars, I can confirm that The Impostor Syndrome *is as prevalent with celebrities as it is in the mainstream. This book is right on the money."*

—Gary Bernstein
Gary Bernstein Studios

"Those who want to be a success must read three books, Think and Grow Rich, Jonathan Livingston Seagull, and now The Impostor Syndrome *by John Graden"*

—Don Warrener
Rising Sun Productions

This book is dedicated to my two sons, Alexander and Christopher Graden. You guys have taught me a dimension of love that I never knew existed until you came into my life. Thank you.

Acknowledgements

To the beautiful lady in my life, Janet Nesselroad. Baby, you're the best!
To my friend Scott Kelby for his wise counsel and friendship.

To my hypnosis teachers, Jerry Kein, Dr. Brian Weiss, Will Horton, Bob Brenner, Ron Eslinger, Cal Banyan, and Tom Nicoli.

To my martial arts sensei, Joe Lewis, Walt Bone, and Hank "The Sun Tan Superman" Farrah.
To the MATA and Pro-Star Mixed Martial Arts members for their confidence and support.

To Brian Tracy and Tony Robbins who have both been more than generous with their help.

To Beth Pry who helped me discover The Impostor Syndrome.

There is an old saying that you find out who your friends are during times of stress and, man do I have some great friends. Frank Shamrock, Jerry Jones, Dan Severn, Matt Fiddes, Don Warrener, Mike Anderson, Rick Bell, Sherie Carlson, Ed Houston, Gary Berstein, Dan Austen, Scott Reis, Richard Staude, Tom Sampson, Al Martino, Jeff Smith, Rebecca Lieberman, Dianna Winkler, Jim Talley, Terry Bryan, Paul Reavlin, Ridley Able, Farid Dodar, Jeff Cohen, Joe Corley, John Therien, Tokey Hill, Kathy Long, Walt Lysak, Richard Ryan, Jerry Beasley, George Alexander, George Kirby, Rick Lucas, Greg Smith, Kathy Marlor, Charlie Foxman, Pablo Zamora, Ridgely Able, John Pellegrini ,Gary Tweton, Joe and Jennifer Galea among others who have shown great support.

My fellow writers and publishers have been very generous to me. A heartfelt thank you to Joe Hyams, Cheryl Angelheart, Robert Young, Mike DeMarco, Bill Bly, Rod Spiedel, Paul Clifton, Alfredo Tucci, Maurice Elmalem, and YK Kim.

To my partner and friend, Joe Brignoli.

Finally, to my sister Dana, and my parents, John and Susan Graden for their unconditional love and support.

Chapter One

PAUL NEWMAN AND I

I once saw Paul Newman in a TV interview say that he always had the fear that one day someone would push through the crowd, grab him by the arm, and say, "It's over, Newman. It was all a mistake. You're coming back to paint houses."

I understood exactly what he meant. He was describing the underlying fear that you don't deserve your success and/or that someone is going to discover that you are a fraud.

Psychologists call this "the impostor syndrome."

I am not a psychologist, nor do I play one in this book. This book is about my personal experiences and the strategies I've used to overcome the self-doubt I lived with for many years.

I thought that once I built a successful business and was receiving international acclaim for my work in the martial arts, the self-doubt would evaporate. Instead, my self-doubt returned with a new name, the impostor syndrome.

The impostor syndrome is the feeling of being a fraud. Regardless of what is going on around you, there is a nagging feeling people will find out that you are not as smart, talented, or skilled as they think you are. It's as though you aren't the person you appear to be to the rest of the world.

The dread that you are to be found out or exposed as being inadequate is always present. This undercurrent of self-doubt makes it hard to strive for excellence because the more you draw attention to yourself, the more vulnerable you feel you are to being unmasked.

Studies in the mid-1980s show that as much as 70 percent of successful people suffered from the impostor syndrome in varying degrees. It's difficult to know exactly how many people have achieved less or never even tried to succeed due to the impostor syndrome.

To me the impostor syndrome is "advanced self-doubt." The impostor syndrome is most prevalent in successful, high-achieving people. Most other people aren't terribly concerned about being exposed because they live low-risk lives.

High achievers risk on many different levels; when that risk pays off and the self-image doesn't match the rewards of the achievement, the impostor syndrome takes root.

We have often observed this in entertainers who work to get to the top and then, once they are there, destroy themselves with drugs and alcohol.

For me, a key realization regarding self-doubt and then later the impostor syndrome is that every successful person "fakes it until they make it." No one has all the answers right out of the gate. But you have to get in the gate to get into the race.

Faking It

One of my favorite programs is a reality show from the United Kingdom called *Faking It*. This show takes someone from one field or background and gives him or her thirty days to learn a new skill and convince experts in that field that they are legitimate.

For instance, they once gave a very conservative young woman classically trained in music a month to learn how to be lead singer for a hard-rock band. A minister was given the same time to become a used-car salesman, and a chess champion was given the task of passing himself off as the coach of a rugby team though he had never played the game or even enjoyed sports at all.

Regardless of the success of the participants in that show, you can understand why they would have self-doubts about their place and position. They fear they will be discovered as a fraud. Paul Newman and I had that same feeling but in real life instead of a "reality show." Regardless of our individual levels of success, lingering self-doubt cast a gray cloud on our clear blue futures.

Faking It instantly recreated the symptoms of the impostor syndrome which include

1. A guilty feeling that you are getting away with something
2. A feeling you're going to be exposed as an intellectual fraud or fake at some point
3. A reluctance to take credit for your success or even say "thank you" to praise

Thought Patterns

Self-doubt has affected my thought patterns since I was a kid. Those thought patterns resulted in patterns of behavior, both good and bad, that defined my life. This book is about how I overcame extreme self-doubt and negative programming.

As you read, keep in mind that all the strategies I share with you have worked for me. I'm sure they will work for you. Essentially, this book will help you to "train your brain." That sounds simplistic, but most of us were never taught how to think; yet what is more important? To be sure, I'm still learning and making mistakes, but I've come a long way; and I'm sure I can help you accelerate your growth.

SELF-CONFIDENCE VERSUS SELF-DOUBT

I know a lot has been written about self-confidence. Here is my perspective on self-confidence and self-doubt. Imagine self-confidence as a positive number. The more confidence you have, the higher the number. Imagine self-doubt as a negative number. The more you have, the farther away you are in the opposite direction.

Here's the good news. As your competence grows in any area, you move from the negative numbers of doubt into the positive numbers of confidence. Here's the reality. Soon after high school or college, most people stop trying to "improve their numbers." That could easily have happened to me, but I don't want it to happen to you.

To say that I was a quiet kid would be understating it to the extreme. I can recall going days without speaking to other kids at school. I felt if I said nothing, I couldn't be teased for saying something stupid.

Bless their hearts, my parents loved me very much and I them; but in our family, the primary training method was to scream when something went wrong. If I did something wrong, it was go directly to scream; do not pass, go; do not ask questions first. After a while, you just learn to be quiet.

On the positive side, the fear that I might be judged as inadequate drove me to study, research, and develop a true hunger for information and learning. As I entered any new field of endeavor, I invested time and money in learning how the best of the best made a success of it; and then I modeled their key behaviors and strategies.

GETTING PERMISSION TO DESIGN MY LIFE

There is no doubt that martial arts played a pivotal role in my gaining the confidence to give myself a chance. From my first karate class on February 12, 1974, I knew I had found my calling. In that first class at age thirteen, I knew this was what I wanted to do for the rest of my life; and I'm still at it. I began teaching private lessons for $7 per hour in 1976. That was great for a sixteen-year-old at the time. I was hired on as a staff instructor for $5 per class in 1978 after earning my black belt.

As my competence in the martial arts improved, my confidence in many areas of life improved. I knew if I could learn to jump over two people and break three boards in the air with a flying sidekick, certainly I could learn to drive a car. Competence led to confidence.

In time, I was on my own, teaching around the area at various community centers and halls. I even taught an accredited college course for a few years, which was ironic because I never graduated high school. I used to joke that I dropped out of high school so I could teach college.

I didn't have to work many hours, and I had Friday through Sunday off. As a young man, I didn't have many needs, nor did anyone expect me to be well-off. I could keep expenses low. So I always had a little cash in my pocket. Being a champion karate instructor brought with it all kinds of social benefits, from meeting girls to being treated like a local celebrity.

However, my friends at the time were following a more traditional path. They were going to college and/or working at jobs they hated. They always seemed broke even though they put in horrendous hours to make any money. They were miserable at their jobs, but I loved mine. They were broke, but I always had some cash to play with. They would tease me about getting a real job, while envying my position.

Eventually, the contrast started to get to me. The impostor syndrome began to develop. I began to feel guilty about this great life I was leading. I started to doubt that I deserved it. One weekend, I was scheduled to fight in a tournament in Gainesville, Florida, and came up a day early to have lunch with a former girlfriend.

Over a nice outdoor meal, I described to her my situation and my growing feelings of self-doubt and guilt.

"I work maybe three hours a day, Monday through Thursday. I make good enough money to get by. On the other hand, my friends are all working forty or more hours and struggling. How can that be?"

She looked me straight in the eyes and said, "John, I know you. You wouldn't accept anything less."

There are moments in life that I call "emotional thresholds." Once you break through them, you begin to destroy the self-doubt related to that area of your life. This was one of those moments for me. It was as though I had permission to design the life that I wanted rather than follow the path of a fresh rat in the race. While it didn't entirely erase my self-doubt, it gave me a surge of momentum in the right direction.

That sense of getting permission to live life on my terms was a huge moment for me, so let me share this with you right now: You, like me, have permission to create the life you want.

As a direct result of my crashing through that emotional threshold on that day at lunch with my friend, I have had a rewarding and lucrative career in the martial arts. I say this because the martial arts industry does not produce a lot of high-income earners. Martial arts schools are usually mom-and-pop labors of love.

THE POWER OF PROGRAMMING

One of my other mentors was an acclaimed plastic surgeon. He told me once that he was a millionaire by the age of thirty-seven. I made a goal to do the same. I beat him by six months.

A key to my transformation from self-doubt to self-confidence was an understanding of the power of programming and self-image.

My friends and I, for the most part, all came from similar financial situations. Most of our families were middle class or lower middle class. "We can't afford that" was a mantra in my home. None of my friends' parents owned their own business that I can recall.

My father was in the army, and my mother worked her way up from a secretary position in a local real estate office to becoming the first female realtor of the year in the state of Florida, which still makes me proud. She didn't lack in intelligence, ambition, or work ethic.

In one of our many meaningful conversations, she taught me that "you have to have a reason to get up in the morning," which still motivates me. Though money, or lack of it, was always a stress in our home, the first wealthy people I spent time with were the successful brokers in her real estate network, which was an early inspiration for me.

My father grew up on the streets of Camden, Pennsylvania, and used the army to help him better his life. He is an avid reader who instilled a love of reading in me at first with comic books. As a kid, I have fond memories of going to the bookstore on Saturdays. I was allowed to pick two comic books and a paperback. Today, at eighty, his table is still piled high with books, which we trade back and forth with the enthusiasm of kids with comics. He also rarely missed a local karate tournament or belt exam and always showed tremendous interest and support of his boy's martial arts training. (Both my brothers are world champion kickboxers. We are the only three brothers to all be individual or team world champions in martial arts history.)

Still, the skills of wealth building and entrepreneurship were like a foreign language to my family and those of my friends. Not necessarily because our parents were against it; but beyond "get a good job and work hard," they didn't really have a strategy for success.

Though we were programmed to follow a traditional path of doing well in school in order to get a good job working for someone else, the fact is that the majority of millionaires are self-employed. You rarely build wealth working for someone else. I heard a great line somewhere. A small business owner puts his hand on his employee's shoulder and points to a big house on a hill and says, "You see that beautiful big home? If you work really hard for me, I can have that one day."

I had two big problems with the traditional path. One, I hate getting up to an alarm clock. Today the only time I use an alarm clock is if I have to catch a plane. Second, I also hated the idea that one-third of my life would be spent doing something I didn't like. That didn't make any sense to me.

Ever since I was a little boy reading biographies of my sports heroes, I wanted to be either an athlete or a teacher. The martial arts provided me with the perfect platform to combine those two passions. Every day, I work at something I love.

My next emotional threshold came when I began teaching. While I knew nothing about business at that time, I did know that I wanted to be the best teacher in the area.

A good friend of my instructor Walt Bone was Mike Anderson, an eccentric genius. Mike used to tell me all the time, "John, you're a great teacher. You should open a school and make a lot of money." As flattered as I was, I knew nothing about making money. I was sure I would embarrass myself trying to operate a business.

Then in 1984, Mike called to tell me that Joe Lewis was in town; and he wanted me to meet him. As a point of comparison, if you are a golfer, it would be like hearing that Jack Nicholas or Tiger Woods is in town.

As a teen, my heroes were Bruce Lee, Muhammad Ali, and Joe Lewis. When my friends and I would play fight, one of us would be Bruce Lee and the other a snarling Joe Lewis. Lewis and Chuck Norris were the biggest names in sport karate.

Mike wanted me to promote a Joe Lewis seminar, which I did. After the seminar, which was a success by everyone's standards, I handed Joe $2,000 in cash and then told him he talks too much in his classes. (Sometimes I feel like I have "truth Tourette's.") The room froze. He looked at me and said, "No one has ever critiqued my teaching before . . ." I'm not sure if that meant "Thanks for the feedback" or "Who the heck are you?"

The next week I asked to spar with him. He told me point-blank, "I don't do that light contact stuff. I fight full contact." I told him I trusted him not to hurt me, and he didn't. We trained hard and often for years following.

The pinnacle for me was when the top martial arts magazine interviewed him and asked who would carry his torch. He named my brother and me. Joe would meet me to spar wherever I was teaching that particular night. One night it would be a basketball court, the next afternoon a college gym or a boxing club. At the same time, I was developing a strong following of students, mostly my college-class students who became "karate addicts." They took my two-hour college class and then followed me to wherever I was teaching to take more classes.

Finally, Joe called me on the phone. "John, you've got to give your students a home," he said. "A place they can take pride in and call their own. If they go off to college, they can look forward to coming home to their karate school."

That was my next emotional threshold. Despite my lack of business savvy, I understood him exactly. I literally lived in my instructors' karate school at times. Most of the time, I stayed all night to train; but sometimes I stayed there to escape my home life. I had a strong emotional connection to the martial arts school as a refuge. The next day, I started looking for a location for my school.

My goal for this book is to use my story to help you understand on a deep level that self-doubt is common even among successful people. We all have self-doubt. What is important is how we handle it. What I'm about to share with you is what I have done to break out of the prison of self-doubt. I realized that self-doubt is self-imposed and self-defeating, but it's as common as a few extra pounds in the waistline. I'm going to help you lose them.

Chapter Two

WHERE THE POWER IN
YOUR MIND RESIDES

*Learning about the subconscious mind is important to destroying self-doubt
and negative programming.*

I f you have ever pressed down on imaginary brakes in a car while you were in the
passenger seat, you have experienced the power of your subconscious mind. Even
though intellectually you know there is no brake pedal on the passenger side, your body
instantly reacts as though it were driving. That is the subconscious mind at work.

TWO MINDS

Each of us has two separate and distinct minds. They have different functions, and
sometimes they have a hard time interrelating and communicating with each other. Some
call this the left and right brain. The way I like to think of them is to imagine an outer
mind and an inner mind. The outer mind is the conscious mind that thinks, analyzes,
and rationalizes.

For this discussion, the conscious mind does four tasks:

ANALYSIS

First, the conscious mind analyzes. Typically, it quickly compares what it is experiencing
now with what it has experienced in the past. This part of the mind analyzes problems
for us and tries to solve them. The analytical portion of your mind makes hundreds of
decisions each day from the most mundane, like which shoes to wear, to the more critical,
like how to pay for your kids' college.

SHORT-TERM MEMORY

The second function is our short-term memory. Short-term memory helps you find your car keys (most of the time) or remember what your dog's name is and your address. This function helps us get through each day.

WILLPOWER

The next part of the conscious mind is willpower. Willpower has a tough job to do, and sometimes it just doesn't get it done. If you have ever tried to will yourself to stop smoking, stop overeating, stop overdrinking, or start exercising, you have discovered the limits of willpower.

Willpower is important, but it may be more important to understand what breaks it down. In recovery programs, they use the acronym HALT to help patients be aware of the fragile nature of willpower and to stay vigilant. Each letter stands for a dangerous physical or mental state in which your willpower is far more apt to crumble.

Hungry: Nothing sends a diet packing faster than hunger. If someone has not yet altered his patterns of thought and behavior on food, he will not have the strategies in place to deal with hunger while on a diet. He will typically relapse into eating as fast as possible, which more often than not means fat- and sodium-packed "fast food." That's why the old adage is to "Never go shopping when you are hungry."

Angry: When people get angry, they act impulsively. They may use that anger as an excuse or justification for relapsing into bad behavior. My friend Dr. Will Horton calls this the self-sabotage attitude of "I'll show you! I'll kill me!"

Lonely: Like anger, this sad state weakens willpower and, like anger, can provide a false excuse for abandoning a healthful course.

Tired: When you are tired, you don't think straight. You make mistakes. The very nature of willpower is the strength to resist an urge, but your strength is weakened when you are tired.

RATIONALIZATION

The fourth function of the conscious mind is rationalization. We know all about this one. I call it the excuse maker. Overweight people say they eat because they are bored. Smokers say they smoke because they need it to relax. Whatever we are trying to stop doing, we find an excuse to do it "because . . ." That is rationalization, and it can be destructive to your growth if you let it. Remember that none of it is true. Rationalization is a dangerous game you are playing with yourself. As the old saying goes, "The only person you are fooling is yourself."

The Subconscious Mind

Your inner mind is the subconscious mind. The prime directive of the subconscious mind is to preserve and protect the body. However, its method is not always rational. Phobias and other irrational fears are an example.

What Is Real?

Irrational fear often occurs when the relationship between respect and fear get out of balance. For instance, consider the difference between respecting the power of the ocean and its creatures and fearing them. Most of us respect the power of the ocean and are careful about how we work and play in or around it. When that respect crosses over into fear, we're moving from rational respect into irrational fear.

When the movie *Jaws* was released in the mid-1970s, many viewers developed an irrational fear of going into the water. Yet had a shark ever attacked them? Of course not, but the fear they experienced while watching the film pushed them from respect of the water to fear of a shark attack.

Films are wonderful because they can penetrate the conscious mind and take us into a state where the subconscious mind doesn't know the difference between reality and imagination. Even though you know that the film is nothing more than light projected onto a screen and everything you see on the screen is faked, your subconscious mind still records the fear. Since one of the main jobs of the subconscious mind is to protect, it pushed some *Jaws* viewers' respect for water and sharks to a level of irrational fear. As far as the subconscious mind is concerned, that fear was associated with water. The subconscious mind doesn't make a distinction between what is real and what is not.

That's why people with irrational fears often say, "I know it's silly, but . . ." Consciously, they know it's irrational. But because the fear was installed in the subconscious mind, it's difficult to get over it in the conscious state. It often requires a process on the subconscious level to correct.

Learning Fear

Virtually, all fears are learned. According to experts, babies are born with two fears: fear of loud noises and fear of falling. The more you allow fear to control you, the smaller your world becomes. In one of the most astounding cases of agoraphobia (fear and avoidance of open spaces and public spaces) that I can recall, a woman stayed in her bathroom for two years simply because she was afraid to come out. She sat on her toilet for so long it had to be separated from her body with a pry tool. For two years, her world was that small bathroom and toilet.

The world opens up to you to the degree you can overcome your fears. One of the most common fears is a fear of rejection. Any parent knows that this is a learned fear because children certainly have no fear of asking for what they want over and over again regardless of how many times they are rejected.

CONFLICTING GOALS

As adults, the fear of rejection often creates a ceiling of potential in many areas of life. When I teach a seminar on sales and marketing, I encourage attendees each day to call the people who have contacted them but have not yet purchased. Many of the attendees get excited about this new source of potential business. However, when Monday comes and they are in the office, they will come up with any excuse not to pick up the telephone and make the call. Why? On an intellectual level (conscious mind), they understand the benefits of making the call. However, on an emotional level (subconscious mind), they have a rule that says they do whatever they can to avoid rejection. The subconscious mind almost always wins these types of conflicting goals, which means the phone calls do not get made.

HOW FAST CAN YOU COUNT?

A friend of mine, Cameron Teone in Los Angles, is a dating guru. He teaches guys how to approach and date attractive women. (You can get a copy of his e-book at TheImpostorSyndrome.com.) One of the first techniques that he teaches is to go out every night for a month and approach at least five sets of women. (Attractive women tend to go out in groups). By the end of the month, you will have approached at least 150 sets. He says the goal is to learn to master the first thirty seconds, and then the next thirty seconds, and then the next thirty seconds until you are comfortable approaching anyone and maintaining control and composure.

At first, making these types of approaches is a nervous, conscious effort. By repeating the process over and over again, the approach gets easier until it is driven down into the subconscious mind where it becomes almost second nature, much like riding a bike or driving a car.

The first time I drove a car, it felt like a disconnected tank. Every movement was a conscious effort. Now, I often arrive at locations and can't remember actually driving there. That's because my subconscious handled the driving while my conscious mind worked on whatever it was I was thinking about at the time.

Here's a fun way to illustrate this. Time how fast you can count to forty-five. Usually it takes about eight-nine seconds. Now, count to forty-five again; but this time, count by threes and time it. Usually it takes about eighteen to twenty seconds. Even though there are twenty less numbers to count, it takes twice as long to count them. You've counted by ones so often it's an unconscious effort. Counting by threes, however, was a conscious effort; and it took twice as long even though there was just one-third of the numbers to count.

YOUR 24/7 RECORDER

When you sleep, your conscious mind rests. However, the subconscious mind quietly works 24/7 beneath the surface like a computer. When you are born, your "computer" was virtually empty. It didn't have an operating system. With every experience, feeling, influence, touch, taste, sound, sight, and feeling, your operating system begins to program you. Some programming is fine while other programming may be harmful in the long term.

Keep in mind that the subconscious mind's job is to mold us into the person it perceives us to be based upon the programming. If your dad repeatedly told you that you were stupid when you were young, you began to believe your programming and acted accordingly. You became your programming. Your programming creates your self-image and your model of the world.

Your subconscious mind is like a full-color, full-sound security video camera that is recording everything you have ever seen, heard, felt, tasted, smelled, or experienced. In the Jim Carrey movie, *The Truman Show*, his character's life was recorded 24/7 by cameras all around him. The subconscious mind is the opposite. It's a nonstop camera recording everything from the inside.

Many experts believe we never forget anything. That's why in hypnosis, clients can be taken back to early times in their lives; and they literally re-experience the event. This is not recall but revivification, during which you see, hear, smell, feel, and experience the event all over again.

EMOTIONS

Emotions make up the next part of the subconscious mind. In fact, one way of looking at the two minds we've been discussing is that the conscious mind is the thinking mind while the subconscious mind is the emotional mind.

The key to influence is making an emotional connection with your audience. Ronald Reagan is remembered as the Great Communicator because he was a master at making this type of connection. He would convey a belief or conviction in just a sentence or two. Once he was asked how he is able to make this connection. He answered, "When I speak to the American people, I imagine that my seven-year-old grandson has fallen off his bike and scraped his knee, and I'm there to comfort him." That's a powerful example of making an emotional connection. He didn't go into an intellectual explanation of how to speak in public. Instead, he painted an emotional scene that instantly told the story. The power of the story bypassed the intellectual mind and appealed directly to the subconscious, emotional mind.

People who can change your emotional state are the most influential and highest paid on the planet. That's why leaders, entertainers, and athletes are paid so much money. They create inspiration, excitement, and powerful emotions.

Emotions are not usually voluntary. Have you ever had a broken heart? It's such a strong emotion that it can actually feel as though your heart is broken. But it's not an intellectual decision. You don't go into your conscious mind and say, "I'd like a broken heart and severe chest pain, please." Emotions pierce the conscious mind whether you like it or not. Just ask any adult male who has welled up during a movie.

PROTECTION

The next component of the subconscious mind is that it protects us or at it least tries to.

My hypnosis instructor, Gerald Kein of the Omni Hypnosis Center, tells the story of a client who came to him for weight loss. She was five feet one inch tall and weighed about three hundred pounds.

Though she said she had an eating problem, Mr. Kein's instincts were that eating had little to do with her problem. He suspected that an event in her past had caused her subconscious mind to protect her by making her heavy. He put her into hypnosis and regressed her to the first time she had the feeling that was associated with this problem.

He discovered that at age six her stepfather had abused her. Though she told her mother, the mother didn't believe her. The six-year-old felt as guilty as though she had done something wrong. This, combined with a few other incidents, led her subconscious mind to conclude that men hurt women so it protected her by having her gain weight rapidly.

She became obese, and men no longer paid any attention to her. That's not the best way to protect against potential predators, but that's how the subconscious works. Protection is one of its key jobs.

Mr. Kein helped her to understand that she was not in any real danger. Over the course of the next couple of years, she lost nearly two hundred pounds. She didn't have an eating problem; she had a problem that had festered for decades in her subconscious mind. Hypnosis is wonderful for this kind of release.

HABITS

The next domain of our subconscious mind is our habits. We all have good habits and bad habits. We also have automatic behavior patterns we don't even think about. Which shoe do you put on first? How do you get into a car? When you shave, where do you start? These are automatic habits you do the same way every day without thinking. It's estimated that the average person spends 88 percent of each day in automatic behavior patterns.

TRUE MIND POWER

Why is learning about the subconscious mind important to destroying self-doubt and negative programming? While intellectually your conscious mind might fully support your goal of creating more positive belief systems and improving your patterns of thought and behavior, you can now see the difficulties of making changes on this outer-mind level. In order for real change to take place quickly and with fewer struggles, we have to bypass the conscious mind and work directly in the subconscious mind.

There are a number of ways to do this. Hypnosis may be one of the best options, which is why I've included a hypnosis session you can download from theimpostorsyndrome. com/readers section.

In addition to hypnosis, we're going to do some exercises that will help you to attach strong emotions to your negative belief systems. In order to drive the process down into the subconscious, there has to be some significant emotion attached to it. This is what I did for years to reprogram myself for success.

Chapter Three

WHO PROGRAMMED YOU?

Understanding programming is important because it helps you understand why people act the way they do.

In front of the ten thousand spectators at a huge martial arts event in Milan, Italy, Japanese karate master Hidy Ochai took a piece of paper and sliced through it like butter to demonstrate that his samurai sword was razor sharp. I was sitting on a chair right in front of him on the stage. As instructed, I laid down between two chairs. Once I was stable, an apple was placed upon my throat. Now that I was in place, an assistant tied a blindfold around Master Ochai's eyes. He reached out to feel exactly where the apple was located on my throat.

Ochai raised the sword high over his head; and with a swift downward cut, he sliced the apple on my throat twice in a fraction of a second. I had allowed him, sightless, to swing a deadly, razor-sharp samurai sword at my throat. Why would anyone give permission for that? I had been programmed to do exactly that.

I'M A BELIEVER

As a young karate student, my instructor told me he had held an apple in his mouth while another black belt blasted it out with a nunchaku weapon, which is a wooden flail that creates incredible speed and power on impact. He could have had his jaw broken and his teeth shattered, so I asked him, "Why would you do that?" His response was, "I'm a believer."

As an impressionable teenager, I wanted to be a black belt like him. On a subconscious level, I immediately programmed that mind-set into my brain. If he was going to believe, so would I.

Looking back, I think it was insane for both of us. There were times when other "believers" did in fact get their teeth knocked out, but that story works as a great example

26

of how an authority figure can instantly reprogram the belief system of someone who is receptive to their input.

TABULA RASA

Aristotle is widely considered to be the first to offer the idea that the human intellect "is like a clean tablet on which nothing is written." He referred to this as "tabula rasa" or "unwritten slate." The idea is that you are born as an empty slate; and your influences, experiences, and authority figures "program" you in your formative years. While there is little doubt that certain instincts, sexuality, intellect, and genetics play a role in development, programming is more about how you are conditioned to view the world.

Every day it seems we hear of religious fanatics blowing up themselves and innocent bystanders in the name of their religion and other strongly held beliefs. While religious diversity exists in countries allowing such freedom, the fact remains that one's religion is strongly influenced (programmed) by parents and other authority figures and location. Not many Christians are being raised in Afghanistan.

Imagine five children born at the same moment but in five different locations: Thailand, Iran, India, Israel, and America. As adults, each one most likely will believe in the teachings of Buddhism, Islam, Hinduism, Judaism, and Christianity, respectively. You could say each was given a different program concerning religion and his eternal future.

Some of these programs are so deeply ingrained and diametrically opposed that their followers have been killing each other for centuries.

WHO ARE YOUR PROGRAMMERS?

Here's what's interesting about programming; the programming was installed without our permission when we were children.

The imaginary five children had no say in where they were born or what religion they were taught. However, each would grow up to believe their religion to be the true religion and, in many cases, to be willing to die for that belief. Many stake everything on their belief.

So who is your programmer? Or rather who are your programmers? We all have many programmers. For most of us, programming comes from our family, teachers, clergy, doctors, friends, the media, good and bad role models, our community, the economic circumstances of our upbringing, and in general, our good and bad experiences and influences.

Understanding programming is important because it helps you understand why other people might act the way they do. This doesn't mean you condone their actions or even like them; but once you understand that we are all products of our programming, it helps you to place the actions of another in a larger context.

For instance, maybe your parents taught you that if you didn't clean your plate, you were being wasteful. Or that you must clean your plate because there are starving children in some poor country. They had good intentions but a skewed message. What if you were full and content after eating only half the food on the plate? Their programming was to ignore your body's natural signals and eat until the food is all gone or feel guilty about it.

If your parents never praised you, you may have a difficult time accepting praise from others. After all, if your parents never said it, it couldn't be true, could it? This is the type of programming that can lead to the impostor syndrome.

THE LONG-TERM EFFECT

What is the long-term effect of that particular programming? For many people, there is not much effect; otherwise, a large percentage of our population would be overweight. Hmmm . . . Maybe that's not such a good example (or maybe it's a great example). Either way, for some people, such programming results in a lifetime of overeating and obesity.

Most advice and programming are well intended, no matter how bad it is. But it's often in direct contrast to the truth.

For example, a parent may say to a child, "You can do anything you want in life, but it's too late for me." A child may hear a parent complain each day about management or the government and ask, "Who's looking out for the working man?" Over time, the programming is that a person has no control of his destiny, that you just get a job that you don't like and get on with it. However, that does not have to be true.

THE TOP THIRD, MIDDLE THIRD, AND BOTTOM THIRD

In every community, there are people who earn the top third of income, the middle third, and the bottom third. A person's current level of accomplishment generally reflects his or her level of ambition, self-worth, and self-confidence. If you went from nothing to something, then you have done something worth sharing. You may have something to teach.

However, many people go from nothing to a little or from a little to a little more. Certainly, there's nothing wrong with that; just don't complain about how little you have. It's not the government's fault. It's not the economy. It's no one's fault but your own. You are the sum of your decisions, and the driving force or fear behind those decisions is often your programming.

What kind of programming has a woman had who took a waitress job at the local diner right out of high school and is still there twenty years later? Who programmed her about building a career and getting ahead? Usually, it's someone with similar programming as hers.

A LINEMAN FOR THE COUNTY

When I was in my early twenties, my roommate, who was three years older than me, kept up a constant lament over his job at the phone company. He was a funny, intelligent, and

28

charismatic guy. But he envied my typical day. I usually slept in until about ten, went to the beach to run, took a nap or took in a movie after lunch, trained at the karate school in the afternoon, then showered and taught at school for a few hours before going out and chasing girls half the night.

His day began at five in the morning, getting up for a job he hated. I asked him what he really wanted to do. He said he'd like to either teach karate like me or go to Disney World and become a performer. I noticed, however, that he already had an attitude of resignation about his situation.

His father had been, as the old song says, "a lineman for the county" for decades; and my friend had been programmed to believe that such work was a "real job." As each year went by, he adopted an older man's persona. He seemed beyond his years, not in wisdom, but in a tired sense of defeat. Today, thirty years later, he still works paycheck to paycheck for the phone company. His health is poor, and he continues to suffer from hardening of the attitudes. The constant financial stress finally came to a head in 2008 when he had an emergency triple bypass. He is recovering well and is looking forward to being able to retire in three years from the phone company. I hope he makes it in good health.

Cultural Programming

Some of us deny we can be programmed. But take, for example, media programming. The media spends billions to program us. Many of us think we are above the white noise of advertising, but we are not. For instance, why would you buy an SUV, with gas prices so high? Are you really back roading that much these days?

Something or someone influenced you to make that purchase, regardless of your rationalization.

Of course, our culture programs us throughout our lives until or unless a paradigm shift occurs. The women's liberation movement was a rejection of past programming that, while important, significantly disrupted the family unit in this country and added massive pressure to women. Today, women are pressured to abandon their role as mother, which leads to another menu of programming, as more children are raised in day care centers instead of homes.

The shift from the conservative traditionalists of the '40s and '50s to the baby boomers of the mid-1960s was huge. The music, the sexuality, the questioning of authority signaled a massive rejection of the programming of those early eras. Of course, all it really did was replace that programming with a newer, more confused version. The Utopian ideals of a free-love-and-peace society never reached fruition. Instead, it left in its wake broken promises and divorced families. But at least the music was great.

Programming Exercise

1. Who were your primary programmers?

2. How would you describe your programming for

   a. Money
   b. Fitness
   c. Relationships
   d. Success

3. Has your current programming served you well?

4. What might you want to reprogram moving forward? Why?

Chapter Four

YOUR HARD WIRING

DISCOVERING YOUR NATURAL STRENGTHS

We know that the impostor syndrome is an underlying feeling of being a fake and the dread that you will be found out. In this chapter, I'll address another identity mismatch that creates tremendous frustration until you take the step I'll describe. This step will align your true self with your daily actions. Stay with me here; this is really good stuff.

We've discussed programming and the idea of Aristotle's blank-slate theory. There is another component that plays a big part in manifesting the real you. There are two processes involved in this component. The first is the cognitive process, which has to do with your conscious, intellectual mind. This is the process of thought, reason, judgment, analysis, comprehension, and other intellectual activities.

In contrast is the process of conation. Conation has to do with your natural drive or inclination to do something.

Your wise decision to purchase this book was, on the surface, a cognitive decision. You considered the price and the content and decided to buy. Thank you. Underneath that decision was a conative process. Like me, you like to learn and research. You have a natural inclination toward learning. So do I. There are many intelligent people who have purchased this book. There are also many intelligent people who would have no interest in buying this book or any other book like this. What's interesting is that both groups are following their natural tendencies.

It's important to discover what your natural tendencies are so that you can align with them. It's also important to know what you naturally tend to avoid and have little, if any, inclination toward them. I was first exposed to this concept in my early forties, and it helped me to change my life rather than my identity.

By discovering my natural tendencies, I was able to stay within the activities that I was strong at and delegate those that I am not strong at. For instance, as an entrepreneur,

I tend to be a visionary and not a detail person. I enjoy starting new projects and feel compelled to jump-start my ideas aggressively. Often, I will have invested both time and money into an idea only to discover that it isn't going to work out.

In contrast to that, I know people who would never rush into a project without thoroughly planning in detail what was going to happen. In some cases, they would discover in the planning stage a flaw or missed component that makes the project undoable. They wouldn't start the project without detailed planning whereas if I had to sit down and plan in detail, I would never get anything done. I am not a detail guy. I have never written a business or marketing plan, and I've owned a half dozen successful businesses. Rather than try to change my natural tendencies to become more detail oriented, I align myself with people who are more detail oriented than me. In this case, we are both working in our strongest areas. You could say that I make the mess, and they clean it up.

We all have natural drives and inclinations for each of these activities/categories. On a scale of one to ten, how would you rate yourself in each of the following categories? One means you tend to avoid the activity, whereas a ten means you have a strong inclination toward it.

1. Risk Taking/Quick Start (Risking resources, starting new projects or ideas quickly)
2. Research/Fact Finding (Researching and learning about new subjects)
3. Detail/Organization (Details, statistics, organization, minutia)
4. Hands-on Implementation (Mechanical, how it works, repairing, building)

For instance, someone who is extremely uncomfortable taking risks would rank a low one or two for risk taking. This person is usually more content as an employee being directed with clear boundaries and security rather than risk. Conversely, a ten risk taker would be miserable in that situation. This person prefers a high risk to reward ratio and enjoys the risks of entrepreneurship and being self-sufficient.

As you can imagine, most people are not on the extreme of either end of the scale but tend to fall somewhere between.

I have a pretty high risk tolerance. I've day-traded (there is nothing like the sick feeling of losing $70,000 in fifteen minutes), skydived, bungee jumped, walked across hot coals, spoken before thousands of people, and fought in full-contact world championship matches. I have not been anyone's employee since 1980. I know other people who have never been anything but an employee and wouldn't have it any other way. Sure, they dream of the kind of money you can make on your own, but they are more drawn to security than risk and independence.

I also enjoy researching topics that interest me. I love to learn. Yet I know many people who dread seminars and others who have not read a nonfiction book since high school. But despite my love of learning, I do not have a detailed mind. Go deep into statistics or finances, and I go deep into sleep.

I am terribly unorganized, which has caused me no small amount of stress through the years. I've taken countless seminars on organizing your desk, life, office, closet, and everything else. In contrast, I have friends and colleagues who are obsessively organized. My ex-wife used to say she likes to have "everything in its own little box," where I was more like "shove it into the closet."

I despise fixing things and care little about how they work. When I go on the car lot and the salesman opens the hood to show me the engine, it is a waste of time. I have no interest in how it works. I just care that it works.

My son, Alexander, is the complete opposite of me in that department. Ever since he was old enough to push buttons and turn switches, he has been obsessed with finding out how things work and fixing them if they don't.

This goes way beyond the natural curiosity of a little boy. His mom and I would regularly ask him what switch turns which light on or how to get the pool pump to work. At age five, he could (and would) tell you exactly how many times to pull the cord on a ceiling fan to get it to any speed. Within ten minutes of checking into a hotel suite, he knows every switch, the AC temperature, and the settings for every fan, as well as how the TV remote works. He has an extremely high inclination for hands-on implementation, which is the opposite of his flesh-and-blood mother and father.

Here is why this is important. These inclinations were not programmed into you. This is your natural tendency. When you know what your natural conative abilities are, it becomes easier to place yourself in position to play to those strengths and outsource your weaknesses. It also helps you to be a more effective and influential communicator. I know that if I'm working with a detail/organization person, I want to feed them facts and figures and avoid high concept vision.

Until I learned this, I can't tell you how many frustrating meetings I had with staff where I would come in excited to share this vision of a new idea, only to have it shot down. Typically, the financial people were the worse. Who are good financial people? They are highly detailed and organized. A great example is when I created *Martial Arts Professional Magazine*. I had this vision of a glossy, full-color, high-quality trade journal for the martial arts industry. Others had attempted it, but their magazines were newspaper print and clearly agenda-driven rags that no one took seriously. I sat my team down and shared this idea.

Everyone was for the idea except the accountant who advised against it as being too expensive with an uncertain return. I ignored her and moved forward with the project. The magazine was a huge hit; and within a single year, it added millions of dollars to our annual revenue and made me the most influential leader in the industry.

If I were to have a meeting like that now, I would not have invited the financial people in until the project had moved along and gained some momentum. In truth, the financial people talked me out of a number of similar projects that I'm confident would have done as well, if not better, than the magazine.

I learned about this concept of conative abilities while attending a strategic coaching seminar through the Dan Sullivan organization. They had us all take the Kolbe A index test which is a measure of your conative abilities.

Taking that test and learning of these abilities was one of the most liberating moments in my adult life. This exam is used to determine where you rank on a one-to-ten scale in each of the above areas. Remember, getting a high or low score is not good or bad, but an indicator of what you avoid or are attracted to in each category.

> My scores were
> Risk Taking/Quick Start, 7
> Research/Fact Finder, 6
> Detail/Organization, 3
> Hands-on Implementation, 3

The conclusion was that my "natural advantage" was entrepreneur. What this did for me was amazing. It made it okay to be unorganized. I wasn't being lazy; it was just not natural for me to spend hours organizing files or doing financial statements. It was fine not to care how things worked or not to be able to hammer a nail straight.

I was liberated from any more "how to organize your life" seminars because the lesson is that once you know your natural strengths, you can spend time maximizing those areas.

My research and risk taking scores indicated that researching and launching projects is what I am good at, and this is where I am going to get the best result and highest returns. I could spend all day each day trying to be more organized and hands-on, but I would never be more than mediocre at either. Yet I could pay someone a fraction of what I earn who will be ten times better at keeping me organized than I would ever be at it.

This helped me in my day-to-day process because I now outsource organization-and detail-oriented projects to people who score high in follow through and organization. For $10 an hour, a virtual assistant will spend three hours creating a spreadsheet comparing postcard-printing estimates for me. I'll spend fifteen minutes reviewing it to make a decision as to which company to go with. Had I done it myself, it would have taken me twice as long with results not nearly as good as hers.

If you manage people, get them tested on the Kolbe A index. In fact, have your family tested so you can know how to best communicate and work with each other.

PLACING YOURSELF AND OTHERS IN A POSITION TO SUCCEED

Once you know what each team member's strengths and weaknesses are, you can more effectively match them to their duties. For instance, in a meeting regarding a new project, the highly organized financial person is usually counterproductive in the stage of the meeting where you are sharing your vision for this new project. Their minds don't work on broad vision; they work on micro details like what's it going to cost? Where are the resources coming from? What's the profit margin?

On the other hand, the high risk taking/quick start person will help you flesh out the vision and contributes enthusiasm to a good idea despite the risks. In this case, you would know to meet with your high risk taking/quick start people in the first half when you are still working out the overall vision of the project and leave the detail/organization people out of that portion of the meeting.

Once it's time to start crunching numbers, excuse the risk taking/quick start guys and bring in your detail/organization team for that section. The risk taking/quick start people will not be interested in the detail/organization section of the meeting, so excuse them from it. Conversely, the detail/organization can cast a damper on a new project with micro details, questions, and concerns that may be premature in the development process. Detail/organization people have a hard time conceptualizing something that has missing pieces or ideas that are not yet developed. They are usually not comfortable in exploratory discussions so leave them out of them for the time being.

Learn more about the Kolbe A index test and take it online at theimpostorsyndrome.com/tests.

Chapter Five

THE CONVERSATION OF A LIFETIME

At about age five, you began an ongoing conversation or a running dialogue that will last your entire life. This will be the most important conversation you will ever have, as it will greatly influence who you become and where you go in life. This conversation is with you.

Over time, nothing is more influential over your ability to give yourself a chance to succeed and overcome the impostor syndrome than your self-talk. Indeed, self-talk and self-image are closely entwined. You become what you think about most of the time.

Few of us are taught how to talk to ourselves. Sure, authority figures tell us to "think positively." What the heck does that mean? Rarely does anyone follow up that advice with examples to help you understand how to frame your thinking into a positive thought pattern. That's probably because the advisor doesn't really know how to "think positively."

THE FROZEN SELF-IMAGE

There are a number of dynamics to self-talk as it relates to self-image. As you grow up, you have good and bad experiences, sometimes really bad. These events, especially the negative ones, can have the effect of "freezing" your self-image at that age.

You may have a number of self-images that you speak with each day. This doesn't mean you have multiple personalities but that you have various versions of you giving yourself advice from different ages.

For example, imagine that at an impressionable age you saw, heard, or experienced something that convinced you that you were unattractive. Or picture a thirteen-year-old boy who overhears his mother talking about how disgusting sex is. The sexual identity of that thirteen-year-old could well freeze at that point. For the rest of his life, his inner dialogue and self-image regarding sex may be framed completely around that single

36

comment he overheard from an authority figure. His mother inadvertently programmed him to believe that women think sex is disgusting.

Because his self-image and self-talk regarding sex are frozen at age thirteen, for the rest of his life his decision making regarding sex may be based upon advice from that confused teenager of years before rather than the mature self-image that is his current age.

Had he heard that same conversation at age twenty-three, odds are it would have had little effect, other than maybe to help him better understand the relationship between his father and mother.

Conversely, a fourteen-year-old girl may hear her father speak of women in a manner that programs her to believe that her worth is tied to her ability to sexually attract men. Her self-image may freeze there and then be supported throughout adulthood by the ongoing conversations in her head with that fourteen-year-old.

In fact, this was the subject of the book *Playground: A Childhood Lost Inside the Playboy Mansion* by Jennifer Saginor. Her father was a famous Hollywood plastic surgeon who is *Playboy* founder Hugh Hefner's best friend. Her father would treat her like one of the guys and critique the look of women on the street. It was in this environment that Saginor and her sister, Savannah, got their first impressions of sex and how men and women relate to each other.

It's not unusual in weight-loss sessions for the client, often a woman, to describe how she sat in the kitchen while her parents yelled at each other. The fighting made her sad, so she continued to eat to make herself feel better. Her view of food changed from its being something to eat because she was hungry to something that provided her with comfort. Food became a friend. From that point on, her inner dialogue regarding food was framed and driven by that sad and frightened little girl.

One weight client was raped as a young teen. Her mother, in a sincere attempt to console her, told her that it happened because she was too pretty. Overeating for the next twenty years was the victim's way of making sure that never happened again.

CHASING THE DRAGON

Immature self-image is often a factor in drug and alcohol abuse. In addiction counseling, the phrase "chasing the dragon" refers to the ongoing attempt by the addict to return to those initial pleasurable experiences of getting drunk or drugged. They want to relive those moments.

Even as their lives fall apart around them and intellectually they understand that drinking and drugging are ruining them, they continue to chase the dragon. The part of them that says to drink is trying to return to that first buzz.

KIDS AND BILLS

A less acute but common example is the messages of our childhood authority figures. When I was a kid, my parents fought constantly; it was clear that in my family the two biggest sources of stress in life were bills and kids. I remember being fifteen and getting yelled at for reading a book at the dinner table because I was using electricity.

The message for me was that kids are a burden, so it's not surprising that I grew up not wanting kids. As an adult, when my couple friends would tell me they were going to have a baby, my reaction was always the same, "On purpose?" I couldn't imagine wanting kids.

For me, that started to change in March of 2000 when I returned from a two-week seminar touring Sydney, Australia. My then wife Lynette seemed very anxious. She explained that she had been all over town buying pregnancy tests. All eleven tests came up positive. We were going to have a baby. Knowing my feelings, she was understandably scared to death.

As the months drifted by, I continued to struggle with the idea that I was going to be a dad. All I could think about was losing my freedom and being burdened by this little kid.

My wife saw this and wisely asked a friend of mine, Scott Kelby, to speak to me about how great being a daddy was. Scott was my first art director. He is one of my best friends and a guy I've learned a lot from through the years. At the time of this story, I was teaching him how to kickbox in my home dojo.

After the workouts, we always went for a walk to cool down. It was during one of these walks that he helped me to understand how great fatherhood would be. He totally reframed my thinking on the subject of children.

My self-talk had been with the adolescent part of me that thought kids were a burden who would rob me of my freedom and eat up all my money. Scott helped me realize that the greatest gifts I could ever have are my children. I never looked back.

The day Alexander was born and later his brother Christopher are the best days of my life. Those beautiful, wonderful, amazing children moved me to a dimension of love that I never knew existed. I am forever grateful for them being my life and for teaching me so much about what is really important while we are here.

In fact, Scott was so moved by my transformation that he wrote a book about me called *The Book for Guys Who Don't Want to Have Kids*. (2005 Peachpit Press ISBN 0321334280)

I think there were several reasons why Scott was able to reprogram my self-image that day. For one, he was a guy I respected, so I listened to him.

Secondly, I observed what kind of daddy he was. A few years earlier, we were working very closely on a daily basis. I distinctly recall the day he told me that he and his wife Kalebra were going to have their first child. I actually said, "On purpose?"

In retrospect, I'm embarrassed at how rude a question that was. However, it serves as a great example of my cocky teenager inner voice speaking on behalf of a thirty-seven-year-old man.

Over the months after Jordan was born, they used to bring him into the office. At first, I was not happy about that. I thought, how are we going to get anything done? Since I was conditioned that kids were a burden, I could only imagine that a baby had to be a worse burden. This set me up for one of the most important lessons of my life.

The first day baby Jordan was in his little playpen in the office, he knocked something over and started crying. I instantly tensed up because in my experience, a crying kid led to screaming parents. Instead, both Scott and Kalebra laughed and comforted Jordan. I couldn't recall ever seeing that before, and it was a huge lesson for me. So in addition to being someone I respected, Scott was a great daddy; and I saw that.

Finally, on the day Scott spoke with me about fatherhood, we had just finished working out; and our endorphins were still flowing pretty good, which may have put me in a receptive state for his words.

Whatever the reason, Scott's conversation took my self-talk regarding kids from that of a confused teenager to my current age at the time. It rapidly began to mature my self-image. That's not to say I didn't still have work to do and lessons to learn. Fortunately, I have two great teachers in my sons.

Up until that lesson with Scott, I thought I had a pretty good handle on my self-talk. Through my martial arts training and the influence of my long-distance mentors like Brian Tracy and Tony Robbins, I learned that my outer world was a reflection of my inner world. I learned that my success was my own responsibility and that the rest of the world had problems and programming of their own to deal with. If it was to be, it was up to me.

Your internal conversations are indeed the conversations of a lifetime: your lifetime. These conversations string together to form your patterns of thought which in turn lead to your patterns of behavior.

Chapter Six

PATTERNS OF THOUGHT AND BEHAVIOR

Consistent, subconscious patterns of thought lead to the patterns of behavior that define your life.

Once you understand the power of self-talk and get your inner voices up to your current age, you begin to understand that the results of your self-talk have been expressed in consistent patterns of thought and behavior over the years. Patterns of thought lead to the patterns of behavior that define your life. We've all heard the saying, "It's not what you say, but what you do that matters." Your patterns of thought and behavior define your life.

YOUR MODEL OF THE WORLD

A pattern of thought is how you view the various opportunities and challenges of your life. Road rage is an example of a negative pattern of thought. A five-second delay sends one person into a horn-honking fury while another person sees the delay as simply a part of the driving process.

Your patterns of thought lead to patterns of behavior. The road-raging driver may associate the traffic delay with being out of control while a rational person realizes that delays are as much a part of driving as stoplights.

Phobias are an example of extreme patterns of thought. A phobic person associates an irrational fear with situations that others find harmless.

Jealousy is also an unreasonable thought pattern. A friend of mine had to get out of the real estate business because her husband was so jealous that if she had to show up home after 5 p.m., he would accuse her of meeting men. He told me once, "If your wife is out after 5 p.m., what the hell are you supposed to think?" This was a man who would not consider the possibility that he was being unreasonable.

Jealousy is especially difficult to deal with because trust can't be proven, only disproved. The jealous spouse is on a quest to prove his or her suspicions. I had a girlfriend once who would go into jealous fits over the most harmless situation. I was watching a football game with her when, during the break, the camera zoomed in on an attractive cheerleader. My girlfriend looked at me, grabbed a pillow, hit me with it, and ran out of the room crying. She screamed and threw things for hours.

When I finally calmed her down some six hours later, she couldn't recall what set her off. I certainly wasn't going to remind her. I did, however, get her to counseling, which helped her immensely. Mind you, it didn't help me because we broke up shortly thereafter. But some lucky guy has a better-adjusted, beautiful girlfriend or wife now, thanks to about $1,000 in counseling paid for by me.

PATTERNS ARE NOT A CONSCIOUS CHOICE

What's important about these patterns of thought is that they are not on the conscious level. Someone doesn't intellectually engage in road rage or fear of flying. Thought patterns are subconscious which makes them even more powerful. Consistent patterns of thought that a person is not even aware of are at the root of self-doubt. This is also why it's so difficult to make changes. It's hard to change something you may not be aware exists, after all, you've been thinking this way for a long time. It feels natural.

Most people try to change their behavior on the conscious level. For instance, going on a diet is an intellectual decision to change eating patterns. Diets rely on willpower, and willpower resides in the conscious mind. As we all have experienced, willpower is situational and not that strong.

Your intellect says that if you follow a diet you will lose weight. Why doesn't it work then? Diets are a struggle because they don't deal with your subconscious mind. A diet places the focus on food, but food is not the problem. Your patterns of thought and behavior about food are the problem.

Dieting doesn't alter the patterns of thought that led you to put on the weight in the first place. Until you change the patterns of thought, you will continue to relapse to the poor eating habits that got you into trouble.

SELF-IMAGE IN A WORLD-TITLE FIGHT

As a preteen, I was heavy. When shopping for pants for school, I was always in the "husky" department. I don't think there is a husky department anymore, but it meant "fat kid."

As a martial artist in my teens, I learned about food and the dangers of sugar and empty calories. We were taught a pretty simple nutrition concept that centered on avoiding sugar and keeping our calories low. Because these lessons came to me at an impressionable age from an authority figure, I accepted the programming readily; and it has served me well for over thirty years.

However, regardless of how fit I became as a fighter, my self-image and self-talk regarding my body was "fat kid." I had a friend once refer to it as "fat mentality." Once you are fat, you always think you are fat. That's certainly been the case with me through the years.

In 1985, I narrowly lost the WAKO world championship heavyweight title. It was a round-robin, three rounds per fight tournament against the best fighters from fifty countries. I fought and won all day until the final match that night for the world title against a muscular German. At the end of a hard-fought three rounds, I ran to my corner and put my T-shirt on. I knew I was going to be on TV and in magazines for the announcement of the winner in the center of the ring. Even though I was in the best shape of my life, my body image was still that ten-year-old fat kid.

1985 World Title Match. My German opponent was as surprised as I was crushed. Notice I'm wearing a T-shirt. Though I was in the best shape of my life, I quickly put a shirt on for the decision. My body image was still as the ten-year-old fat kid.

LOSING OVER ONE HUNDRED POUNDS

Thanks to what I've learned through the martial arts, I've developed good patterns for eating; however, I have friends who had different programming about food, which led to patterns of behavior that drove them to overeat. One friend who was well over one hundred pounds overweight had tried every diet from A to Z (Atkins to zone.) He is also one of the most intelligent, well-adjusted, and funny guys you will ever meet. But, as he recently discovered, he associated food with fun.

He loved to go to restaurants with friends and "pig out." He would go into a fast food joint and order a double cheeseburger and large fries with a side of Velveeta cheese to dip the fries in. This, combined with an aversion to exercise, created a walking, talking heart attack waiting to happen.

Fortunately, he began training in martial arts (hmm, I wonder how that happened?), started seeing a nutritionist, and is in the process of reprogramming his patterns. He has lost over one hundred pounds and is on his way to a healthier and happier life. When a guy tells you how excited he is to be back down to an XL shirt, you know he's replaced the short-term pleasure of eating garbage with the long-term pleasure of feeling healthy again.

What happened? He just got sick and tired of being sick and tired. He broke through an emotional threshold that instantly reprogrammed his patterns about food. His old pattern of associating pleasure with overeating was, in reality, bringing him massive pain. The short-term gain of eating something he enjoyed resulted in the long-term pain of carrying around an extra one hundred pounds.

The change for him came when he took the focus off food and found out why he was overeating. That's when he discovered that he associated food with fun. Now he has reprogrammed himself to associate food with nutrition and to associate overeating or eating unhealthy foods with pain.

GETTING YOUR BUTTERFLIES TO FLY IN FORMATION

How about the problem of approaching someone you are attracted to? You can change your outer world by getting into great shape, dressing better, and improving your looks; but in many cases, it's like painting over a rust spot. The rust is still there. Your self-doubt still fuels a pattern of thought, "He or she won't like me. What if he or she rejects me?"

Those butterflies swirling in your stomach don't come to you intellectually. They emerge on the subconscious level. That's why the experts say the best way to approach is instantly. In his book, *The Game*, Neil Strauss describes the three-second rule, by which you must approach within three seconds of seeing the woman you are attracted to. Your subconscious mind doesn't have time to push self-doubt up to the conscious mind. I call this technique getting your butterflies to fly in formation.

Patterns of thought are the result of our programming. They are usually installed early in life without our knowledge or permission. They formulate our belief systems. For instance, most of us have pretty strong beliefs when it comes to a higher power. Odds are those thoughts roughly reflect those of our parents and the community we grew up in. Parents usually don't expose us to several religious belief systems and allow us to choose. The serious nature of this type of belief includes a strong desire that their children share the same convictions.

MONEY CHANGES EVERYTHING

Thought patterns concerning money are also strongly influenced by our parents and other authority figures in our formative years. Given a similar lower- or middle-income background, education, and intelligence, what causes one person to break out and become a financial success while his or her peers repeat the history of their parents? One difference is that the successful person rejects many of the thought patterns that the circumstances of his upbringing attempted to install.

If you notice, I used the example of lower- and middle-income families. Higher-income families are more apt to install patterns of thought that lead to financial success simply because they usually know how to think about money. Those patterns are already established. Lower- and middle-income children are usually taught about money by parents who don't have much of it.

In fact, in many households, money (and often sex) is treated as a forbidden subject. But what could be more important? Parents program their children to believe that the pursuit of money means you are greedy. We're raised to believe that rich people got that way by stepping on the little people, selling their soul, or being born with a silver spoon in their mouth. This creates a tremendous confusion and stress in our society. For instance, have you ever loaned someone money and then were afraid or uncomfortable to ask for it back when they didn't repay it? Why? It's your money. You are certainly entitled to it. The banks don't have a problem making sure you are aware of your debt to them. While you certainly want to be repaid, you have an internal conflict because you've been programmed to believe that asking for money means you are greedy.

You can be sure the media and advertisers understand and play upon this programming. That's why bankers are typically portrayed as heartless, money mongers. (A great example is in the classic James Stewart Christmas film, *It's a Wonderful Life*.) Producers tap into programming to elicit the emotions they want to create in the film.

In training sales people, the most difficult part for most of new recruits to learn is to "ask for the check." Most people can learn the presentation and recite the many benefits of the product or service, but they choke when it comes time to ask for the check.

CREATING WEALTHY PATTERNS

During my childhood, the lack of money was a source of great stress in my family. For me to learn how to attract money into my life and make it grow, I had to study the habits of wealthy people. I had to learn the difference between a financially successful person's perspective on money and that of someone who struggles with money.

I was lucky in two ways. As a young karate instructor, I attracted some wealthy clients as private students. One was a wealthy plastic surgeon who took me under his wing and taught me how wealthy people live. He had a big gold Mercedes that he would take me to the yacht club for lunch in. He took me to tennis and polo matches and exposed me to a world I only saw on TV. He helped me to see the opportunities the world presented.

The other lucky event was when my kickboxing instructor handed me a six-cassette tape audio seminar by Roger Dawson called *The Power of Negotiation*. He said it was boring to him. While he was an intelligent man, he would have rated very low on the Kolbe A index scale for research.

I plugged the tape in; and Roger, in his charming British accent, taught me more about negotiation in a few hours than I had learned in all of my life. I discovered the world of audio seminars, and I was hooked. I resolved to spend all of my weekday driving time listening to these great teachers educate me on how to create wealth and design a life rather than make a living.

I'm proud to say that two of these masters have become friends. Brian Tracy has simply been great to me. He has always supported my projects including serving on the board of my American Council of Martial Arts, and he wrote the foreword to my last book, *The Truth about the Martial Arts Business.* (Seconds Out, 2004.) Tony Robbins appeared on my TV show three times. (Check John Graden interviews Tony Robbins on YouTube.com to see them.) He also provided us with a gratis keynote presentation for my final NAPMA convention in 2003. Gentlemen, I offer a deep bow of respect and gratitude from your faithful student.

I stopped listening to corporate radio drivel and focused on turning my car into a four-wheeled university. The returns for the investment of time and attention have been in the millions of dollars and untold improvement of the quality of my life. Listening to teachers of that caliber and then implementing what you learn will change your life forever. It certainly changed mine. I'm convinced I am a better person, teacher, friend, son, and father as a direct result of nearly two decades of constant learning.

In time I learned to adopt the patterns of thought of ambitious and wealthy people as my own patterns. If you want to be wealthy, learn to think and act as wealthy people do. There has never been more information at your fingertips on how to build the life of your dreams than right now. The fact you are reading this book shows you are taking the right steps to build the future you desire.

ACTION AND BELIEF MATCHING EXERCISE

The key to improving your patterns of thought is to first recognize how you currently view certain areas of your life. Here's an exercise to help you match what you intellectually believe about some important areas of life with your patterns of behavior.

1. Write down your beliefs on the following subjects (you can add other topics if you wish):
    a. Money
    b. Success
    c. Risk taking
    d. Relationships
    e. Exercise
    f. Eating

2. Write down the evidence that your behavior supports that belief. For instance, imagine you wrote that exercise is important to your life and happiness. If your evidence that your behavior supports that belief is that you exercise at least a few times a week, then your behavior and belief are congruent.

3. Look for instances where there is either an inconsistency between your stated belief and your actions or where your belief is causing you trouble in a particular area of life. If you say eating is a way to stay healthy but you are eating a quart of ice cream each night, your patterns are not consistent with your belief. You're not clear on your belief. You might think, intellectually, that food is to keep you healthy; but your true belief, as reflected in your patterns of thought and behavior, is that you view food as a source of pleasure and comfort. That is a belief that will lead to overeating and one that you will want to work on modifying. Here is an example using some of my current beliefs.

My beliefs on the following subjects:
a. Money—Is an important tool for freedom and security.
b. Success—Is my birthright and drives me every day.
c. Risk Taking—Is necessary on all levels in order to grow.
d. Relationships—Are critically important in life.
e. Exercise—Is like showering to me. I feel bad if I miss a day.
f. Eating—Is mostly for nutrition, but sometimes for fun.

Evidence supporting my beliefs or inconsistencies:
a. I save at least 10 percent of my income.
b. Each decade I have pushed myself to new challenges that have the potential to bring higher income and acclaim.

c. From writing a book to stepping on stage or launching a business, I put myself out there on a regular basis.

d. I have a tendency to isolate myself. This is where my self-doubt has haunted me. Intellectually, I understand the importance of relationships. My patterns of thought and behavior are not supporting that as much as I would like, though they are getting better. This is also the area that I will risk the least, so I am working on improving this area.

e. I train almost every day and am in excellent shape. I use a personal trainer twice a week to make sure I'm being pushed harder than I would push myself.

f. Since learning how to eat as a young martial artist, I avoid fatty, sugary foods and have a simple goal of keeping my calorie intake reasonably low. If I have to cut weight, I lower my calories and increase my training.

This exercise works as a reality check to make sure you are "walking your talk."

Chapter Seven

A POWERFUL LESSON ON PERSPECTIVE

Your subconscious mind doesn't know the difference between what is real and what is imagined.

For years, as a young competitor on the Florida karate tournament circuit, I would see Herbie Thompson compete in the black belt fighting division. The circuit was racially charged in those days, with Thompson the respected and feared leader of a group of black fighters from Miami. Though he was respectful and friendly with my instructor, Walt Bone, he was rarely friends with anyone he faced in the ring.

He threw trophies and chairs if he didn't win first place and always seemed ready to explode into a street-fighting rage if things didn't go his way. One time we had a black belt team competition between our school and a team led by Thompson. I was just a brown belt (this meant I was about a year away from testing for black belt) and had settled in to watch what I knew would be a rough, volatile series of matches when my instructor motioned me to come over.

He told me to follow him into the locker room where he pulled out a black belt and told me to put it on. At age seventeen, I had been recruited onto an adult team of black belts. I was terrified.

In the first fight, our biggest fighter got his nose broken six feet out of bounds by a blatantly illegal punch. We got the penalty point, but he got a trip to the hospital. After cleaning up the blood, the next round started; and our best fighter got knocked out of the match with a powerful kick to the back, which nearly crippled him. I was next. I did better than the black belts so far but lost some points.

In the final match, my instructor was up against Herbie Thompson. We were way behind in points, but my instructor regained the points; and we won the team competition. Thompson went nuts. While excluding my instructor from the tirade, he kicked things, spewed foul language, and threw his equipment across the room.

In a sport based upon principles of respect and courtesy, this was disturbing and, in our view, disgraceful. Fast forward twenty years, and we are profiling Thompson for my magazine, *Martial Arts Professional*. What I discovered was a great lesson in perspective.

We asked him about the days when he would throw a tantrum after losing. His response was as revealing as it was unexpected.

We discovered that for over thirty years, including the "old days" when he raged over a loss, Herbie had dedicated his life to using the martial arts to save children in the roughest inner-city communities of Miami from the temptations of crime. He has been a mentor to hundreds of kids and has no doubt saved many lives.

He explained that he would load as many kids into a van as possible and drive them out of Miami on Saturdays to a karate tournament. Some of the kids competed and some watched, but all were out of harm's way for the day. Between the gas and the entry fees, he was out of money by the time the tournament started. If he didn't win the cash prize for first place, he couldn't feed the kids; and he would have to borrow money to get the gas to get home.

His story instantly changed or reframed our perception that he was a disrespectful jerk. In fact, he was a desperate hero to these children, many of whom run their own martial arts schools today.

Is Perception Reality?

The old saying is that perception is reality, but is it really? The answer is yes. Your mind doesn't know the difference between what is real and what is imagined. Your perception is reality until something or someone changes it.

Have you ever walked into a room and jumped when you caught your reflection in a mirror out of the corner of your eye? That is a fight-or-flight response from your subconscious mind. You didn't think, "Oh, that is an attacker. Let me jump into my defensive posture."

No, your mind was confused and instantly got ready for fight or flight. Your heart began racing; and you may have started panting or lost your breath, all in a fraction of a second. Though there was no threat, your subconscious mind didn't know the difference between what was real and what was not.

Maybe you've been working hard and know that you deserve a raise. However, you've had negative programming about money, which resulted in a pattern of thought that asking for money means you are greedy. Rather than asking for the raise, you convince yourself that you'd rather not have the money than be seen as greedy.

This is a pattern of thought that goes to a negative potential outcome before anything actually happens. Understandably, this thought pattern reinforces self-doubt. It's "Why play the game? I'll just lose again."

Your perceived fear dominates the pattern and prevents you from doing what is best for you. A great acronym I learned years ago for this common thought pattern is FEAR.

False

Expectations

Appearing

Real

Maybe you see someone you'd like to get to know better, but rather than introduce yourself, your pattern relating to rejection kicks in; and you convince yourself that someone that attractive or popular probably already has plenty of suitors better-looking than you!

Do you know someone who seems to start each conversation with, "Did you see what happened in the news? It was horrible . . ." This person focuses on bad news, which, over time, begins to frame his or her perspective of the world. Anyone driving faster than her is a maniac, and anyone driving slower is an idiot.

WEAVING NEW PATTERNS

To begin modifying or reprogramming your patterns of thought, become vigilant in monitoring yourself: how you view, respond to, and act in certain situations.

A weight-loss client recently expressed to me how upset she was at her husband. He had allowed an eight-year-old girl to accompany their young daughter into their home one afternoon.

The husband was there along with another father from the neighborhood. However, this woman complained that the little girl "had no business in her house." She was upset because the girl's mom didn't know where she was.

As she recounted the story, she became more emotional and upset. Here is an abbreviated transcript of the conversation:

Me: "What upset you and why?"

Client: "My husband. He was in the house with another man from the neighborhood. Our daughter walked in with an eight-year-old girl that we didn't know. She had no business in my house. Her mother didn't even know where she was!"

Me: "What about her being in your house upset you?"

Client (getting agitated): "My husband should not have let her into the house. In this day and age, she could have said anything. Her mother didn't even know she was there. She had no business being in my house! She could say anything, and we could lose everything!"

Me: "Is she a friend of your daughter's, or did she just walk in off the street?"

Client: "No, she's a friend."

Me: "Is your daughter allowed to bring friends into the house?"

Client: "Not if her mother doesn't know where she is!"

Me: "Is that your daughter's fault?"

Client: "No."

Me: "Is it the girl's fault?"

Client: "She should tell her mother where she is, but she's only eight. I think the mother should know where her daughter is. What kind of mother does that?"

Me: "Couldn't your husband have called the girl's mother to tell her she was at the house?"

Client: "I didn't think of that. Yeah, that would have been good."

Me: "Do you trust your husband not to molest little girls?"

Client: "Of course, but her mother didn't know where she was. She could have said anything."

Me: "Couldn't the little girl say anything, regardless of whether her mother knew where she was?"

Client: "I never thought of that."

Me: "In reality, the fact the mother didn't know where she was would probably work in your favor if something ever was said, because she could be viewed as somewhat negligent."

Client: "You're right. I never thought of that either."

Me: "Can you see how you created distress for yourself and your husband over something that didn't exist? Certainly, you want the girl to be safe, and you know she was safe with your husband. Any little girl can say anything at any time. Your husband was in the house with another man and your daughter. Was there really a threat to be concerned about?"

Client: "When you put it that way, I guess not . . ."

This is a classic FEAR scenario. She created massive stress by responding to a false expectation that the girl might accuse her husband of molesting her. She was so upset because it was appearing real. Of all the possible scenarios, she chose to frame the incident in the most negative. She had a big fight with her husband and was upset for two days before coming in to see me.

A Waste of Stress

For sure, a mother needs to know where their daughters are, and I'm not making light of that at all. But there is a huge chasm between concern for the girl and two days of anger. That's what I call a waste of stress. I believe stress is at the root cause of many, if not all, of our ailments; and disease (dis-ease means the lack of or the lessening of ease) is a direct result of stress. I also believe, and have no way to prove it, that we all have a certain amount of stress "credits" in our lives. When we've spent those credits, we are out of here. I'm real big on not wasting stress. As the old saying goes, "Don't sweat the small stuff." Many people are rapidly spending their stress credits on events that either don't really exist, are beyond their control, or is a remote possibility. If worrying helped, I would ask everyone to worry for my children. It doesn't, so save your stress for something real.

WHEN YOU PUT IT THAT WAY

By walking her through the scenario in a more realistic manner, I was able to help her to reframe the situation. Yes, we'd like for the girl's mom to know where she was, but that didn't really increase the risk factor for her husband in that scenario.

When she said, "When you put it that way . . . ," she was recognizing how I had reframed it. I "put it" in a more realistic frame that was without stress and with little or no risk or stress attached to it. Whereas she had "put it" as the potential to lose everything.

The client learned her negative thought patterns created constant stress for herself and her family.

People with patterns that focus on the most negative possible outcome can delude themselves into thinking they are being responsible when they worry and project that negative energy on anyone who'll listen. In reality, people who frame the world that way are exhausting to be around and, in time, often slip into depression.

The client in the above example is on medication for depression. She framed the world in such a negative way that it came as no surprise that she was a comfort eater. In subsequent sessions, she said she was starting to catch herself framing situations in the negative. She was learning to explore other ways to look at the possibilities rather than embracing the first negative pattern that emerged.

THE FOUR STAGES OF LEARNING HOW TO REWEAVE YOUR PATTERNS

You can work to recognize your own patterns of thought. It's not always easy because they are so ingrained that they may feel quite natural. At first, the weight-loss client had a hard time seeing the situation as anything but "That girl had no business in my house." It wasn't until I walked her through the scenario as described above that she could see other healthier, more positive possibilities. Then she was able to intellectually reframe the situation into a more realistic perspective. With practice, she can begin to reweave her patterns to envision more positive, hopeful scenarios.

Here are some of the techniques I've used through the years to destroy the self-doubt that a negative frame of the world creates. But first realize that all of us go through a learning curve. There are four stages to learning, and you will go through all four in learning how to reweave your thought patterns.

1. Unconscious Incompetence

You don't know what you don't know. It never occurred to the woman described above to pay attention to her patterns of thought and to walk through them to see if her concerns were valid or were false expectations appearing real.

2. Conscious Incompetence

This is where most of you are now after reading this far into the book. You understand some of the roots of your self-doubt and the impostor syndrome and are learning how to eliminate them.

Reading about them in this book brings them to your conscious level, but knowing and doing are not the same. Learning is experiential, and that begins at the next stage.

3. Conscious Competence

You know what to do, but you have to think about it to do it. Reframing and reweaving your thought patterns requires that you monitor your thinking and responses to situations and then think them through to make sure they are valid concerns.

4. Unconscious Competence

Where I want you to get to as fast as you can. At this level, you have been practicing reframing to the point where it happens without your having to think about it. Like driving a car, the actions and reactions take place on a subconscious level and are as natural as your old patterns of thinking were. You've completely replaced your negative framing that seeded your self-doubt with a more positive possibility frame of thinking that releases your potential. This will fuel your growth into being a happier, more successful person.

Understanding these levels is important because it helps you to develop patience and understanding for your progress in any endeavor, including reframing and reweaving your patterns of thought. This helps you monitor your progress in this and anything else you try to learn.

When you don't have a way to measure your progress, it's easy to get frustrated. Frustration, over time, leads to self-doubt, which often prevents you from even trying anything new. Again, "why play the game if you're just going to lose again?"

A progressive learning curve allows you to set reasonable short-term goals and enjoy the satisfaction of hitting them. For instance, reading this book brings the concepts of programming, self-talk, self-image, patterns of thought, and reframing to your consciousness, whereas maybe you never thought much about any of them before. That takes you instantly from stage 1 to stage 2.

Hopefully, the book and audio sessions at theimpostorsyndrome.com will motivate you to practice reframing your patterns of thought, which will move you to level 3. Congratulations! Now, with practice, you are on your way to level 4.

The same principle applies to every area of your life that you are trying to improve.

Most people expect to start at level 4. Then they get frustrated and quit when it doesn't happen right away. The four levels work as short-term goals that allow you to recognize and describe your progress at any time.

Certainly, it's my goal with this book to help you destroy self-doubt and the impostor syndrome so you can give yourself a chance to do better at anything you choose. Using these levels as a progress check will help you a great deal.

"WHAT DID I DO WRONG?"

Have no doubt that you will encounter some speed bumps along the way. You will stumble and fall short occasionally, and that's OK. It's better to be in the race than on the sidelines. Let's just make sure you frame the effort in the best way possible.

For instance, you decide that you are going to increase your income because you have significantly destroyed your self-doubt and are in the conscious competence level of learning how to sell a new product or service.

You make a call on a client, and you don't get the sale. As you drive away, your old thinking might have been, "What did I do wrong?" or "I messed that one up." This kind of framing tends to carry some emotion with it. It's hard to imagine "messing up" or doing something "wrong" and not attaching a negative feeling to it.

I want you to learn from the experience but leave the emotion in the past. Instead of "What did I do wrong?" frame the review this way, "What will I do differently next time?" This puts your mind into the future where your next sale is and pulls the lesson learned from the missed sale while leaving the emotion in the past. We strip the emotion from negative experiences and take the lesson with us into the future.

This makes your speed bumps as valuable as any lesson learned along the way.

Chapter Eight

CREATING HEALTHY BELIEFS

As we mature, hopefully our view of the world changes.

Think of beliefs as powerful tools that you use to create the life you want. In the last chapter, we identified some of your beliefs and did an exercise to see if your patterns of behavior supported your beliefs.

What you do speaks more loudly about your beliefs than what you say. Parents know that too, so many quote the old saying, "Don't do what I do, do what I say," which is another confusing example of programming.*

OUR BELIEFS CHANGE

In this chapter, we want to start to identify belief systems that may be creating the self-doubt that is holding you back. Then we will formulate a strategy to transform those beliefs to more positive, productive ones. This is no easy task because a person can have an enormous range of beliefs, and some beliefs are stronger than others. Also, as we discovered, change is easiest when it's implemented on the subconscious level or as the result of crossing an emotional threshold.

Toward the end of this chapter, we'll walk through a belief-transformation process that simulates an emotional threshold, and we'll give you the step-by-step tools to discard, replace, or modify any negative beliefs.

The very nature of the word "belief" implies rigidity. A belief, by definition, is the acceptance by the mind that something is true or real; and this is anchored by an emotional or spiritual element. If it's one of your beliefs, then that's the way it is; or is it? Beliefs can change, and they do all the time.

Churchill is credited with saying, "If a person in his twenties is not a liberal, he doesn't have a heart. If a person is in his forties and not a conservative, he doesn't have a brain." As we mature, our view of the world changes, as do some of our belief systems.

Indeed the very nature of wisdom is the process of making bad decisions, learning from them, and not repeating them. That's also why it's so important to isolate those various self-images and get them all to the same age so you can benefit from the wisdom of your full life experience, as we discussed in chapter 5: "The Conversation of a Lifetime."

Your beliefs will change throughout your life. Rather than think of them as etched in stone, think of them as powerful but dynamic tools that you use to create the life you want.

Some beliefs work even when they are not true. Did you believe in Santa Claus? I did. For about five years, Santa was real; and he added to my holiday excitement. I didn't feel betrayed when I discovered that he only existed in our imaginations. It didn't matter to me, and I bet it didn't matter to you either.

An animal trainer chains a young elephant to a tree or post, and it learns that it can't get away. He programs the elephant that escape is futile and the chain will always hold. By the time the elephant weighs five or six tons and is more than strong enough to break the chain, his belief is still there that he cannot escape; and he doesn't even try.

Your beliefs can be as strong and as wrong as the elephant's. Remember the story (in chapter 3: "Who Is Your Programmer?") about the weight-loss client who was very pretty but about seventy-five pounds overweight. Her hypnotherapist regressed her in hypnosis to the first time she felt the feeling that brought her into the office that day.

She regressed to a terrible incident at age seventeen when a schoolmate raped her. This was in the 1970s; and rather than go to the police, her mother simply told her, "It's because you are so pretty." In a misguided way, her mother was trying to make her feel good about herself. She developed the subconscious belief that "If I am pretty, this may happen again." Overeating was a way to make her less attractive.

That powerful belief system had tremendous negative effects on the quality of her life. It was not even a conscious belief. She was in the office for a weight-loss session. Still, her subconscious mind held on to that belief and prevented her from succeeding with any attempts at losing the weight.

That's why we did the exercise in chapter 6: "Patterns of Thought and Behavior." Your conscious mind may think you believe a certain way; but your actions tell you more about your true belief systems, which are stored in your subconscious mind.

So what negative beliefs are creating self-doubt for you? Following are fifty examples of negative beliefs. This is by no means a complete list; but as you read it, mark any that you feel you might be carrying, and then add to the list any other negative beliefs that you might have.

Fifty Examples of Negative Beliefs:

In order to be attractive, I must be wealthy.
In order to be attractive, I must be in perfect shape.
In order to be attractive, I must have a full head of hair.
In order to be loved, I must put others' needs first.
I must be perfect.

I'm inadequate, inferior.

I'm a loser.

There is something wrong with me.

I'm different.

I'm too old.

I'm too young.

No one will ever love me.

Asking for help is a sign of weakness.

When people give me a compliment, they are just trying to make me feel good.

If I think I can't do something well, I won't try it.

I always have to know what I'm doing or else I feel I should quit.

What other people think of me is important.

I'm the only one I can count on.

Making mistakes is a sign of stupidity.

I won't succeed, so why bother trying?

I'm not worthy to be equal to others.

If I speak up, they will discover I'm a fake.

It's my fault that my sister (brother, friend, etc.) died.

My opinion isn't worth anything.

I don't deserve to be happy.

My thoughts and feelings don't matter.

I grew up poor and undeserving.

I come from a freaky family; we deserved to be shunned and ostracized.

Expressing my emotions is wrong, or it means that I'm a weak person.

I'm stupid for feeling this way.

No one cares about me.

It's better to harm myself physically than to feel the emotions I've repressed.

I must please people for them to like me.

I have to be in control of every situation.

It's best to let someone else be in control of the situation.

I shouldn't upset anyone.

It's selfish to stand up for myself.

Relaxation is a sign of laziness.

Doing what I like is selfish.

I have to do everything, or nothing gets done.

I always have to be on the lookout for something bad.

Worrying about people shows them I care.

Telling people what to do shows I am smart.

The world is a very unsafe place.

Even if someone seems to like me, when they really get to know me, they won't like me.

Having a clean, orderly house shows I am a good person.

I have to make people around me happy.

I make people sad, happy, and angry when they are with me.

I don't like myself; why should anyone else?

I didn't graduate high school/college, so I'm not smart enough to . . .

As you review your list of negative beliefs, take them one at a time and break them down for a reality check. When I've done these exercises, I've used pain and gain as my measuring sticks.

PAIN AND GAIN

Typically, a negative belief or bad habit will provide a short-term gain but also burden you with long-term pain. Ice cream each night sure can taste good for the short time you are eating it. However, the long-term effects will be feeling unhealthy, not fitting into clothes, being judged by your waistline, and feeling bad about yourself.

Our goal is to reprogram and reframe your patterns so that you are comfortable with the opposite thinking, which is short-term pain for long-term gain. Skipping that ice cream and having an orange may be at first be a short-term pain, but it will result in the long-term gain of being in control of your body and looking your best. The more you can associate pain with a negative belief or habit, the easier it is to replace it with a new belief that will bring you long-term gain.

Staying home and studying or working instead of going out and partying may be a short-term pain, but the long-term gain will be a more successful career.

Spending twenty minutes exercising is a short-term pain that results in huge long-term gains.

Keep in mind that the more you practice new positive patterns, the activities will not really be a pain at all. You will grow to desire the great mental and physical feeling of a good workout. Your body and mouth will reject ice cream and bad foods and crave healthy food instead.

All work and no play does make Jack a dull boy, but all play and no work makes Jack a broke boy. Doing what needs to be done when it needs to be done is not as difficult as it sounds. In fact, you gain a great feeling of momentum when you know you are doing the things that most people are not willing to do. That's the very nature of "getting ahead."

Here are some questions to challenge negative beliefs:

1. What hard evidence do I have to show this belief is working for me?

For instance, "It's selfish to stand up for myself." How do I know? Did someone tell me that? If someone did, who was it? Why did they say that? How do they know? What authority are they in the area of standing up for oneself? Could they be mistaken? If it's selfish for me, then it must be selfish for everyone. How does anyone then justify standing up for himself? Is everyone who stands up for himself selfish? Is it right that everyone but me should be able to stand up for him or herself? Over the years, has not standing up for myself caused me more pain or gain?

I bet you get a short-term gain of having an excuse not to stand up for yourself, which has resulted in long-term pain.

2. What strategy can I use to help me replace this negative belief with a more productive one?

Now that you see that not standing up for yourself is causing you long-term pain, use that realization to propel the transformation. Begin to associate pain with keeping quiet, lots of pain. This doesn't mean becoming a hypersensitive blowhard; it just means to develop a strategy for speaking up for yourself.

As someone who has battled shyness all his life, I spent a lot of time finding the right words to say in situations like this. When someone either said something or did something I objected to, I had a hard time standing up for myself. The impostor syndrome convinced me that I wouldn't say the right thing or that I was not as deserving as anyone else.

Here's a good strategy that has worked well for me. It will work for you too and give you momentum to change the belief, especially when you start to enjoy the benefits of doing so.

When someone says something that I feel I need to stand up to, I say, "Maybe I missed something, but that doesn't seem fair to me. Let me see if I'm clear on this . . ." Then I restate what they said and explain why I don't think that's fair. I don't attack them or tell them they are wrong.

If someone does something that I feel I need to stand up to, I say, "Sir, I'm sure you didn't mean to cut in line . . ." This way you are giving them the benefit of the doubt rather than being confrontational.

This is borrowed from the Japanese martial arts of aikido principle of align and redirect. Rather than confront the person, you align with them. "Let me make sure I'm clear on what you said . . ." and "I'm sure you didn't mean to . . ." are examples of aligning with someone and then redirecting them to understand and respect your point of view.

3. How can I now reframe this belief to help me instead of hinder me?

This belief: "It's selfish to stand up for myself," can now be reframed to, "I have the right to stand up for myself and the obligation to my well-being to do so."

Standing up for myself is just one of many patterns of thought and belief systems that I have personally worked on through the years to improve my life and destroy my self-doubt.

Very early in my adult life, I knew that freedom was an important value for me. I wanted to do whatever I wanted to do with whoever I wanted. I wanted to make my life, not make a living. In our culture, freedom is purchased with dollars. I realized in the mid-1980s that I would have to sacrifice freedom for a few years in order to gain decades of freedom later.

For instance, as I mentioned in the last chapter, I stopped listening to the radio. It's important enough a lesson that I want to take a moment and expand on the impact it had on my life. It started with creating a negative association with commercial radio. I began to associate listening to the radio with a corporate machine sucking money and brain cells from me. How many hours of your life have been sucked away listening to commercials on the car radio? How many songs you don't really care for do you have to sit through to get to one you like? How many hours of talk radio consists of hosts repeating what everyone else is saying that day or even worse, reading the day's events to you off the wire?

We live in a world of information overload. My mind goes 24/7 anyway, so I don't want it burdened with the drivel that flies through the airways each day.

I turned that dead driving time into active learning time. My car became my "success university" on wheels. Rather than listen to brainless babble and commercials, I listened to Brian Tracy, Roger Dawson, Denis Waitley, Tom Hopkins, and other success coaches. I remember Brian Tracy saying over and over, "If you study a subject an hour a day, you will become an expert. In five years, you will be a national expert." That had a massive impact on my thinking patterns and belief systems.

When I started listening to these guys, I went from unconscious incompetence to conscious incompetence on the learning scale. Within a few months, I was at level 3, conscious competence. Within a year, I was at level 4, unconscious competence. Now I teach this material worldwide. Thank you, Mr. Tracy. I would never have learned that important lesson, along with countless others, if I were listening to 98 Rock like everyone else I knew.

I don't think I have purchased a newspaper in years. I have not read one article about a child being killed or some awful tragedy that editors pass off as news. I don't want that negative information in my life. Awful things happen every day to someone. That doesn't make it news; that makes it life.

The lessons I learned from those masters changed my life positively in many ways. It hasn't always been easy; but day by day, I chipped away at my self-doubt and created a new set of beliefs that have continued to evolve with me.

Fortunately, I've continued to work and challenge myself to the point that some of my masters have become my friends and colleagues.

I tell you this not to brag, but to inspire you to realize that what I'm teaching you works. It's worked for me, and it will work for you. But you have to do the work.

Chapter Nine

LIFE IS PERFECT

How to create light at the end of your tunnel.

As I sit here and write this book, I can reflect on some great events in my life: earning my black belt; the birth of my children; building a business that changed an industry I care deeply about and improved the lives of tens, maybe hundreds of thousands of people; and having a career that is rewarding in every way.

At the same time, a wealthy man who seems intent on my financial destruction filed multiple lawsuits against me personally. He said he sues me to "keep me out of mischievous activities." That's some interesting programming for you. Over the past six years, this has cost me my business, all of my savings including my children's college funds, and contributed to my wife divorcing me.

Guess what? Life right now is perfect. Not preferred, perfect. Perfect is different from preferred. That doesn't mean life is fair. It means life is a mixture of good and bad for everyone.

Imagine you are floating above your city at about ten thousand feet, just looking down at your community. What is happening? It's kind of hard to see, but you do observe that the area is alive with people and movement. To get a better look, let's float down to about three thousand feet. Now you can see houses, buildings, and cars. What you see is life.

As you look down on that community, babies are being born, some people are laughing, some are dying, some are crying, some are making love, some are being abused, some are studying, some are sleeping, and multitudes are engaged in a myriad of other activities.

You are seeing life; and while you are looking at life, you know that from birth to death, at any given moment, people in your community are experiencing the full range of good and bad. That is life. Each time you hear the siren of an ambulance screaming by, you know that someone is having a worse day than you.

That is a macro view that can be drilled down to a micro view of your own life or mine. Our lives are a mixture of good, bad, and everything in between. It's what we choose to focus on that determines our outcome.

STRIPPING THE EMOTION FROM THE PAST

The most successful people are able to turn the negative events in their lives into lessons that will accelerate their recovery and success. One major difference in how successful people and people who struggle view the past is in what they attach to a past event. Successful people either strip the emotion from a negative event or take forward only the lessons learned, or they use the emotion and pain of the event to propel them forward.

Sports psychology shows that athletes who expect to win are more apt to do so than those who don't. When a successful athlete wins, he or she takes responsibility for his performance. When losing, he or she will often place the blame on other factors beyond their control, such as the wind or officiating.

Conversely, when less successful athletes win, they are less apt to take credit. Then you'll hear comments like, "I got lucky today." But when they lose, they take full responsibility. They have the reverse mind-set of the successful athletes. Often, this is the impostor syndrome in control. The message is that if I take credit for this, you may expect me to do it again.

WHAT HAPPENS TO YOU DOESN'T DEFINE YOU

People who struggle tend to hold on to the negative events of the past. Instead of disassociating from what happened, they cling to it. One of the realizations I made after getting blasted with lawsuits and a sad divorce is not to let those events define me.

Quite easily, I could have thrown in the towel, opened a karate school, and literally retreated back in time. But I spent years developing the programming, thought patterns, and strategies I'm discussing in this book. There was no way I could allow myself to bail out. Having a positive attitude is easy when things are going well. However, the better you get at creating a positive outlook and approach to life, the better things go, even when they don't go so well. Dreams are not built upon pessimism or cynicism.

When you are able to reframe your world into a "life is perfect" perspective, you begin to see more clearly the lessons life offers you. It's my belief these are lessons we're meant to learn from as we develop as humans. This mind-set helps you develop a curiosity about what is happening around you and to you.

Throughout the devastating lawsuits mentioned above, many friends asked me how I handle it so well. My answer is that it's been a fascinating process to lose my business, my marriage, and my savings. Usually, their response is that, "fascinating" isn't the "f-word" they would use to describe it. I just tell them that this has taught me a lot about myself and how others respond to you when you are in a situation like this.

The situation continues as I write this book. In fact, it is the inspiration behind this book. I would not have written this book nor anchored so deeply the lessons it teaches had I not been going through this stress.

I went from living debt free in a million-dollar home with a high six-figure income and $600,000 in the bank and over six figures my children's college funds. Life was good, and then the lawsuits began. The general impression was that I had become too influential in the martial arts. In particular, I began to suggest that the standard white karate uniform (gi) was an unattractive outfit for beginners to have to wear. The standard karate uniform was the staple product of my wealthy antagonist. He decided to take me out and he did.

Five years, three or four lawsuits (I've honestly lost track), and one amicable divorce later, I was $800,000 in debt with about $15,000 in bills per month. Defending that many lawsuits wiped me out financially. My kids' college funds were empty. I could have easily filed for bankruptcy and given up.

There is a lot more to this story, and none of it is pleasant; so let me just say that I am back to debt free and on my way to rebuilding and resecuring my children's future.

There is no doubt that the success of my rebuilding process is a direct result of the lessons in this book. They worked for me, and they will work for you. Resilient optimism is not about being happy-go-lucky in the face of negative events. It's the ability to create your own light at the end of the tunnel.

A Lesson From Ali

Imagine a spectrum of day-to-day optimism and happiness. The more optimistic you feel about your future, the happier you are. For this illustration, imagine the peak of that happiness; and optimism is at the number 100 on this spectrum. At the other end of the spectrum all of the way down to the number 1 is the more pessimistic end of the spectrum.

Let's say right now you are at a fifty-five. You are somewhat optimistic about your prospects, and that makes you feel pretty good. You start to apply the lessons from this book; and you teach yourself to move up the spectrum of optimism and happiness all the way to an eighty, which is great. You feel more confident about your future than ever before. You're feeling happier about your life; and you can see that the ceiling of self-doubt is rising each day, allowing you to reach for higher and higher goals. You're on your way, and it feels good. Maybe for the first time in your life you feel you are in the driver's seat of your destiny.

Then, because as we know, life is a mixture of good, bad, and everything in between, you get laid off or divorced or have some kind of setback that challenges your attitude. For a period of time, you might get down or lose some motivation; but in fact, this is what you have been training for. Like a fighter, you don't train hard to win the easy fights. You train hard for the times you are in the ring, blasting your opponent with your best shots; but he takes it and smiles in your face.

This is the battle I faced, and this is exactly what happened to Muhammad Ali in 1974 when he fought the heavyweight champion, George Foreman. Foreman had destroyed everyone he fought up until this fight. Even greats like Joe Frazier and Ken Norton, who each gave Ali all he could handle, crumbled in front of Foreman.

Ali came into the first round with a strategy of leading with the right hand. This is a very powerful but dangerous punch for the puncher because it takes longer for the punch to travel to the target than a jab. It's also rather insulting to the other fighter to lead with the right because the message is he is too slow to do anything about it.

Foreman was such a devastating puncher that no one led with the right hand against him. He hit so hard a fighter couldn't risk getting counterpunched, so he would be more careful and predictable. Not Ali. He took the fight to Foreman and threw sixteen lead rights in the first round, and many of them scored. Some smashed so hard that sweat exploded off Foreman's head. For the most part, Ali's strategy worked in the first round. His right hand scored and frustrated Foreman. There was a little problem, though. Ali had hit Foreman with his best punches, yet Foreman didn't go down.

Ali returned to his corner in a fighter's nightmare: He was facing a bigger, stronger, and meaner opponent who had just taken his best shots and stayed in the fight.

Ali knew this was the test for him. In the seconds between round 1 and 2, he realized that this was why he had trained so hard. All the training came down to this moment.

He knew his initial strategy hadn't worked, but he had trained so hard that he was able to draw upon backup strategies. In this case, he reversed his game plan from being the aggressor to playing possum.

He leaned back on the ropes and let Foreman blast away at him. In effect, he was saying, "Give me everything you have because I am in great shape. I have trained my mind and my body to deal with this punishment, and when you least expect it, I will conquer you."

For the next seven rounds, Ali took ferocious punishment. Through it all, he encouraged Foreman to hit harder. He taunted him, "George, you're letting me down." "I thought you could hit hard. That's it?" Foreman went berserk, punching as hard as he could until, in the eighth round, he was so tired he became vulnerable to Ali's right hand. Ali knocked him out in one of the greatest upsets in boxing history.

After the fight, Foreman went into a deep depression that lasted for over two years. Eventually, he pulled himself up and returned to the ring to recapture the world title and become a multimillionaire entrepreneur.

Foreman completely redefined himself and his patterns of thought and behavior from a brooding bully to a charming champion, commentator, and pitchman.

Yes, it's easy to have a positive attitude when things are going well. It takes the tough times when your attitude, outlook, and beliefs are put to the test that you get the payoff.

Going back to the spectrum analogy, when something challenges your attitude, you may drop back on the spectrum to a seventy or even a sixty for a little while. But you're still more optimistic about your future than you were back when you were at fifty-five with only a pedestrian attitude about your life.

Certainly, things happen that are beyond our control, and they may make creating the life you desire difficult. The best strategy is to create the best life you can with what you have. Setbacks are rich learning experiences that you and I can take forward. Designing the life you desire is very much dependent on your ability to transform your negative experiences into positive lessons.

Lessons Learned Exercise

1. What have been your major setbacks or obstacles?

2. How did you deal with them?

3. In retrospect, is there anything you have done differently?

4. What are the lessons you can pull from them moving forward?

Chapter Ten

Setting New Strategies

"The world needs ditchdiggers too!"

There is a great line in the classic comedy *Caddyshack*. The main character is a young golf caddy who comes from a poor family. While caddying for the chairman of the golf club, he remarks that he would like to go to college; but his family doesn't have the money. The chairman's cold response is, "The world needs ditchdiggers too." And he is right.

The world offers more opportunity today than any time in history. Yet by nature many people take the path of least resistance and then blame the government, their parents, the economy, or anything else for their situation. But in truth, they have failed themselves by their choice of life strategies.

One evening before teaching one of my karate classes, I watched two women practice a pattern of techniques called a kata. Kata is a traditional series of precise movements. One woman walked through the kata with full execution of each technique. She extended each kick, block, or punch the full range of motion in excellent balance and stance. The other woman was looking up, clearly trying to remember the moves. She did each movement about halfway and never fully completed a technique.

Later I asked each student, "What goes through your mind when you are practicing?" The first said she wanted to practice as closely to correct form as possible. The other woman said she just tried to remember the moves. Over time, which student do you think would excel?

The women had different strategies for practice. The precise student was precise in many areas of her life and eventually won a world championship. The other woman never made the effort to excel at anything and, incidentally, always struggled with her weight.

We all have strategies for almost everything we do. As we have learned, these strategies are not conscious but learned patterns of thought and behavior. If you can discern your own strategies, you can modify them to get better results. If you adapt and effectively execute the strategies of someone who is experiencing success in a certain area, you too will improve in that area.*

What Is Your Strategy?

A common example for personal strategies is in weight control. If you wanted to gain lots of weight fast, you would do what? Eat like a fat person. When an unhealthy, overweight person sits down in a restaurant and looks at the menu, she uses a very different strategy in choosing what to eat than a more health-conscious person. She looks for something to eat based upon how it tastes, with little regard to the effect the meal may have on her health. If she is with a friend, she might use a justification strategy: "I know I shouldn't, but these fried cheese appetizers are so good." She orders appetizers, a meal, and then dessert, all based on taste. This is also a typical comfort-eating or taste-eating strategy. She is choosing what her mouth wants rather than what her body needs.

She chooses the short-term gain of a tasty meal for the long-term pain of being fat, unattractive, and in poor health.

A healthy person's strategy is to determine how much she wants to eat and then find the healthiest options and choose from them. She starts with, "How hungry am I really? What looks healthy?" She looks for something in the healthy category that tastes good to her.

As time goes by, the strategies for the healthier eater are going to result in a healthier lifestyle and a fit, toned body.

How are your strategies serving you? How is self-doubt affecting those strategies?

Let me share with you the strategy that changed my life. This was first taught to me by Brian Tracy as "delaying gratification." Later, Tony Robbins summed it up succinctly as short-term pain for long-term gain, which is how I view the strategy now. Pain, in this context, is defined as varying degrees of discomfort and inconvenience. That doesn't sound too appetizing at first, does it? It will be finger-licking good once you understand it!

Humans are, by nature, lazy. That's not good or bad; it's just the way we are. In fact, most all innovation is designed to make things easier, faster, and more convenient. Given the choice to do something the easy way or the hard way, it's human nature to do it the easiest way. This natural tendency can often work against your best interest. However, the fact that most people take the easy route can also work in your favor, provided you don't follow their example.

Here's what I mean. Most people choose the short-term gain of avoiding the risk of trying something new and, by default, endure the long-term pain of underachieving in their life. Rather than risk the potential of failure, they would rather not try in the first place.

The common strategy among a majority of the population is short-term gain for long-term pain. They stop trying after high school or college and accept their place in the rat race. This is self-doubt in action on a large scale.

Four important examples of accepting short-term gain for long-term pain are

1.   Staying in a job that does not challenge or compensate you like you deserve.

Go to a restaurant or hotel and see people who have been working there for a decade or longer. It's not unusual for these people to complain about the government and how it "should look out for the working man . . ."

They have many complaints about their situation, but they simply take no action to improve it. When a young woman calls you "sweetie" as she takes your order, you get the feeling she is resigned to being a waitress for life. She is already adapting the mannerisms, thought, and behavior patterns of the older waitresses who began this same pattern twenty years earlier.

Her decision to avoid the short-term pain of striking out for greener pastures will result in a lifetime of financial pain for herself and her family. Her family tree is negatively affected by her reluctance to try.

2.   Discontinuing education.

It's amazing to me how reluctant people are to learn new skills.

As I mentioned earlier, Brian Tracy's greatest lesson to me was, "Pick a subject you love and study it for an hour a day. In most cases, you will become an expert within a year. Within five years, you will be a national expert and able to sell your expertise."

This was a key strategy for me. I was willing to sacrifice the short-term gain of going out with my friends for the long-term gain of developing the skills I needed to become a millionaire. For successful people, learning does not end with school.

3.   Settling in an unhealthy relationship.

This is often the result of accepting the affections of the first person who comes along and shows interest in you.

This often happens to people who feel a strong need to be in a relationship, not because they care about the other person, but because they don't like to be alone.

You have to have standards in your life. (Attraction is far more than physical, and it is certainly not intellectual. Attraction is on a visceral level.) If you create a strategy of enduring the short-term pain of being alone and not jumping into the first relationship that comes along, you have a much better chance of enjoying the long-term gain of finding someone you can really grow with. The opposite is to risk wasting your life with someone you don't respect.

4.   Spending money.

What you do with money may be the easiest way to measure long-term pain or gain. Money doesn't care what you do with it. Money is like a hammer; you can either build or destroy with it.

Some people use money to build security for their families or a foundation for the poor. Others use it to sue people. Money doesn't care one way or the other. People, who understand money, save at least 10 percent of their income and invest it so it grows over time. They stay out of debt and pay their credit cards off monthly.

People who understand interest collect it. Those who don't, pay it. The short-term gain of buying something you don't need results in the long-term pain of reaching retirement age and being dead or dead broke.

Here are three examples of short-term pain for long-term gain:

1. A doctor endures over a decade of pain attending medical school and interning in order to enjoy a lifetime of prestige and wealth.
2. A person endures the short-term pain of regular exercise and eating smart for the long-term gain of looking and feeling great.
3. A person engages in the short-term pain of saving money and paying off debt in order to enjoy the long-term gain of being financially secure in retirement.

Simply put, the key to success is to delay gratification. It is to resist the temptation of taking the easy way out. It is to associate massive pain with the pedestrian activities of "normal people." Normal is not a group you want to be associated with. You want to be exceptional. You want to associate great pleasure with doing what you need to do to get ahead. That may not sound like fun, but it's true.

During and right after our divorce, my ex-wife Lynette would say, "John, normal divorced couples . . ." And I would say, "Lynette, normal is not a group either of us want to be associated with." In time, she caught on; and we have since been great friends. It's fascinating when people find out that we all go on vacations together as a family, even though we've been divorced for over two years. Especially when they find out that my fiancée comes along and has developed a close friendship with Lynette. It's as though people can't fathom continuing to care about the well-being of the other parent of your children after divorce. I'm not saying the divorce was easy; it was awful. But we both resisted the short-term gain of going after each other emotionally and financially for the long-term gain of seeing our children happy and having each other as close friends for life.

The strategy of short-term pain for long-term gain, when applied in an intelligent manner, is the pathway to success in all areas of life, even divorce. However, most people will not do that. Most people continue to take the path of least resistance or risk. Let me clue you in on a secret: That's good because it makes it easier for you and me to get ahead of them. After all, the world really does need ditchdiggers. They just won't be us.

STRATEGY EXERCISE

1. What is your current strategy regarding

   * Weight control and fitness?

   * Building wealth?

   * Learning new skills?

2. If you are not pleased with your own life strategies, how could you modify them to get better results?

3. Who would be a good person to model yourself after to achieve the level of success that you desire?

Chapter Eleven

YOU ARE NOT ALONE

O ur collective programming is so powerful an influence that marketers have defined segments of the population based upon their values and beliefs, which we know are a product of our programming.

For decades, advertisers have used demographics as a way of targeting specific age and income groups. In addition, advertisers now use psychographics as a way of matching products and services they are selling to the lifestyle values of a particular segment.

Why is a marketing strategy part of a book on eliminating self-doubt? Actually, it's more accurate to say that I am using the millions, if not billions, of dollars the advertising industry has invested in research to help us understand programming and values on a mass level.

So far, we've discussed programming on the individual basis. This chapter is intended to show how large segments of the population share similar programming and belief systems. I think this is fascinating and a lot of fun. I know you will too.

PSYCHOGRAPHICS

Psychographics include lifestyle, social class, and personality traits. While psychographic segments can be drilled down to over a dozen different groups and subgroups, we're just going to focus on six of them.

Once you understand these concepts, you will never watch an ad the same way again. You will see how ads target the pain and pleasure of a specific psychographic group. The strategy in addressing each of these segments is to either move them away from pain or toward pleasure. Each group has its own triggers for personal pain and pleasure.

As you read this overview of the six main categories of psychographic segmentation, see if you find yourself in one.

The Struggler
The Socially Conscious
The Belonger
The Explorer
The Emulator
The Achiever

THE STRUGGLER

Pleasure for the Struggler: Looking tough and rugged, escaping, taking the path of least resistance, and belonging

Pain for the Struggler: Looking weak, change, challenging tasks, and alienation

The struggler has a mind-set of resignation to a hard life. They often have little education and low confidence in improving their situation. They don't believe they have the resources, other than manual labor, to improve their lives. They are heavy consumers of fast food, alcohol, tobacco, and lottery tickets. They do not save their money because they make very little of it and usually have very few money-management concepts. Strugglers are routine oriented and fearful of change. This fear is often rooted in a self-doubt that they have what it takes to handle change.

The struggler is a classic example of the life created by a short-term-gain, long-term-pain strategy. Strugglers take that strategy into every part of their lives from jobs and relationships to diets. They tend to take the first job and first relationship that comes along and then, rather than risk the pain of looking for a better job or relationship, accept the short-term gain of staying in their comfort zone. That results in the long-term pain of a hard life.

THE RICH ARE THIN AND THE POOR ARE OVERWEIGHT

The strugglers' eating strategy is typically to choose what is cheap and tastes okay, which is typically the fattest, sweetest, high-carb, high-sodium fast food. In part, this is why we live in the unusual population dynamic where the rich are thin and the poor are overweight, which is the opposite of historical patterns.

Strugglers find it difficult to set and achieve worthwhile goals. They have a short-term outlook on life. Essentially, the goal is to get through the day. Long-term planning is not typical of the struggler. Strugglers from struggling families often make up young gangs. Strugglers feel the need to break the rules (and sometimes even the law) to survive. Often, because they are surrounded by like-minded people, strugglers use their perceived disadvantaged plight as an excuse for breaking the law. The attitude is, "What other choice do I have?" or "I do what I have to do to survive." Because of this attitude, the world is a small place for the struggler.

(If the description of the struggler resembles you in any way, let me first congratulate you on buying this book. I bet none of your friends have it. Using the strategies in this book will help you move out of this difficult segment of society.)

THE KNOWN DEVIL

For the struggler, the single greatest obstacle to making the changes he needs in his life is his "comfort zone." A comfort zone is the tendency to get into a routine or rut that, regardless of how bad or negative it is, holds you back because you resist the changes necessary to improve your position. As the old saying goes, "The known devil is better than the unknown devil." This is why people stay in abusive relationships or in dead-end jobs. They fear the risk of striking out for a better life.

Strugglers have a reactive mind-set, meaning that they tend to wait for something better to come along; but nothing ever does. Strugglers don't tend to initiate actions to improve their situation or future. They want things to get better by themselves and they won't.

Strugglers must take a proactive approach and take the necessary steps to improve the quality of their life and change their family tree forever.

Change is part of life. Things are changing all the time. In order to improve their situation, people must recognize comfort zones in their life and take the steps to break out of them today. Where are you engaging in short-term gain for long-term pain?

THE EXPLORER

Pleasure for the Explorer: Adventure, hedonism, breaking rules, discovery, cynicism, experimenting, and change

Pain for the Explorer: Routine, rules, sacrifice, convention, blind acceptance, and tradition

The explorer is a relatively new segment of society. Many believe these are the children of parents who were teens and twenty-somethings during the cultural revolution of the 1960s and 1970s.

In a 1969 *Playboy* interview, comedian Don Rickles was asked what he thought about the hippie movement. His response was, "I don't think about hippies. Today's hippy is tomorrow's mutual funds salesman." That Nostradamus-like prediction could not have been more accurate.

The so-called free love generation promised a Utopian world of peace, love, and tranquility but instead delivered drugs, divorce, and hypocrisy. Consequently, many of their children have a mistrustful and cynical view of the world.

The rise in popularity of extreme sports is a reflection of the growth of the explorer mentality. Whereas their parents protested for social change and communal harmony, explorers are unapologetically self-centered. They don't like to answer to anyone or follow convention.

Advertisers appeal to explorers with excitement and rebellion. Smirnoff Vodka had a print ad that is an image of pigeons sitting on the gargoyles of a building. Three gargoyles look the same, but the fourth has wide eyes and a full mouth with feathers sticking out. He broke the rules by eating the pigeon.

CHASING THE DRAGON

Explorers have to be careful with their short-term-gain, long-term-pain approach to life. They will eventually have to grow up and take care of themselves and their families. I think most of us go through a period of youthful exploration, which is probably healthy. But to continue to "chase the dragon" can, in itself, become a limiting strategy because your resources, especially financial, will dwindle in time.

Unless you are lucky enough to earn the riches of a champion skateboarder like Tony Hawk, you may end up selling mutual funds to survive—probably socially conscious mutual funds!

THE SOCIALLY CONSCIOUS

Pleasure for the Socially Conscious: Unconventional thinking, intelligence, freedom, nature, creativity, and independence

Pain for the Socially Conscious: Waste, rules, restrictions, industrialization, abuse of power, closed minds, and conformity

The socially conscious population segment is the idealists. They recycle, drive hybrids, and think green. They tend to be liberal, to volunteer, and to feel that it's the government's responsibility to take care of the poor and needy.

They are suspicious of large corporations and will spend a little more money to support a product or service that reflects their values.

The socially conscious tends to prefer natural, simple products. They take pride in having an antimaterialistic attitude that may or may not be supported in reality. They tend to take pride in their intelligence and in nurturing idealism. Advertisers appeal to the socially conscious by showing that moving forward with them will be for the greater good of society or nature. There are socially conscious mutual funds specially designed to invest in companies that are environmentally and socially responsible.

Like the explorer, the socially conscious took roots in the 1960's western cultural revolution.

THE BELONGER

Pleasure for the Belonger: Routine, rules, sacrifice, tradition, patriotism, belonging to a group, and order

Pain for the Belonger: Change, autonomy, rule breaking, selfishness, lack of patriotism, being singled out, and hedonism

The belongers make up the largest segment of society. These are the working men and women who obey the laws, enjoy belonging to groups of like-minded people, and place a high value on family. The belonger believes that family, friends, and faith are the backbone to a strong society. They are price conscious and save for the future. They belong to unions, bowling leagues, churches, and other groups of belongers. They are suspicious of management and don't like to be singled out.

Belongers, in many ways, are the backbone of society. They do the work that needs to be done; and they work to keep the family unit intact, which is critical to community structure. They help maintain tradition in their routines and beliefs.

Belongers are attracted to products and services that help keep the family together or support the working man ethic.

Here is an example of how an ad is designed to appeal to belongers by creating the pain of a splintered family and then healing the pain with the service they are selling: "During these busy times when the children are off to college and Grandma is across the country, the holidays can be a lonely time. Bring the family together with our low-cost long-distance plan . . ."

THE EMULATOR

Pleasure for the Emulator: Sex appeal, appearing cool, fashionable, looking successful, material goods, being part of the in crowd, and hedonism

Pain for the Emulator: Self-sacrifice, being left out, feeling unattractive, appearing uncool, out of fashion, or poor

The emulators and the strugglers are probably the best examples of self-doubt on a large scale. They are also good examples of short-term gain for long-term pain.

Looking cool and appearing rich motivates emulators. They want the latest fashions, coolest cars, and hippest gadgets. The cooler they look, the better they can mask the self-doubt that is fueling the charade. Keep in mind, there is a difference between being successful and confident and being an emulator. Emulators "emulate" wealthy people. They are not one of them. That doesn't mean they won't be; but more often than not, emulators have a "big hat but no cattle." Emulators want the appearance of being successful without investing the work or time to actually create the wealth they pretend to have. Instead, they go deep into credit card debt. That is a classic short-term-gain, long-term-pain strategy.

PUT IT ON THE CREDIT CARD

Emulators are a great market to sell to because they buy impulsively and with skewed logic. Coors Beer used to run commercials that showed beautiful women in bikinis playing volleyball on the beach. An image of female physical perfection would fill the screen; then she would fade out, and a can of Coors Beer would replace her. The message is drink Coors, get sex. They never mentioned that a girl with that kind of figure doesn't drink beer. That would require thinking. Emulators are driven by basic instincts of attraction, acceptance, and sexuality, not logic.

Their short-term-gain ("put it on the credit card") long-term-pain strategy for life has resulted in a record number of bankruptcy filings for people under the age of twenty-five.

If you are an emulator (you know who you are), make it a goal to get out of debt fast. Have a garage sale and get rid of the junk you have purchased and barely used. Start saving your money and work your way from faux wealth to real wealth like our next segment of society, the achiever.

THE ACHIEVER

Pleasure for the Achiever: Leadership, goals, tradition, control, competition, ethics, innovation, prestige, productivity, and methods of measuring results

Pain for the Achiever: Following, lack of direction, unproductive time, chaos, lack of control, underperforming, and disorganization

The achiever is pretty much everything the emulator wants to be. The achiever earns a six-figure income and is a "leader of men." He or she is competitive, disciplined, and goal-oriented. The achiever lifestyle only happens with a deliberate strategy of short-term pain, long-term gain.

For me as a young person, that strategy was opting to stay in and work rather than go out with my friends. It was creating a system of saving 20 to 50 percent of my income year in and year out.

Many achievers go through rough times, and many go bankrupt. But usually the bankruptcy is the result of taking calculated business risks that go bad. Achievers are willing to risk more because they have overcome self-doubt and built tremendous confidence in themselves.

The achiever attitude was taught to me by Brian Tracy, and it's simply this: If it's to be, it's up to me. No complaining. No whining. Get on with it. Achievers take full responsibility for their success and setbacks. Achievers don't fail as much as they experience setbacks that they choose to learn from and build from. The achiever views these as lessons learned and resets his goals to rebuild.

When I taught karate, I always knew when an achiever was considering joining my school. He interviewed me, more than I sold him on joining. He came in and watched more classes than most prospects. He asked smart questions about the time frame required to earn a black belt and what kind of commitment would be involved.

Tuition wasn't the issue; time and commitment were. Achievers are deliberate in their thinking. They know that if they commit to earning a black belt, or any goal, they will follow through; so they don't want to make that commitment lightly.

Achievers, like all successful people, like to be measured. From their waistline to their net worth, achievers like to know where they are and where they are going.

Achievers think of themselves as unique. They don't like to be grouped with other people. Merrill Lynch once ran a TV spot that showed a group of bulls walking down Wall Street. The goal was to imply the power of wealth; however, the ad performed poorly. When they changed the ad to a single bull walking through a china shop, the ad's response was much higher.

Achievers are still likely to be affected by the impostor syndrome. Since they have worked themselves up the ladder, some still have a nagging self-doubt that they don't deserve their success or that it's just a matter of time before someone finds them out. The difference is that the impostor syndrome drives them to work harder to avoid making any mistake that might reveal their self-doubt.

For me, this was a natural thought in the beginning of my martial arts career because I tried many things that no one else did. Once a famous martial artist introduced me to 1,500 black belts at a convention by saying, "The lead dog gets all the thorns. John Graden has taken a lot of thorns for us all."

I sure didn't start out that way. I remember as a kid being called everything from "Dumb John" to "Chumley." (Chumley was the overweight sidekick to the Tennessee Tuxedo cartoon character.) However, as I mentioned before, I began to study and adapt the learning and thinking patterns of successful people. I began to fake it until I started to make it, and it worked.

In time, I began to see that I was developing a track record of success that was undeniable. Remember, confidence is built upon a foundation of competence. Certainly I had a lot of great help, but those were relationships I put together by hiring the right team or positioning myself with people whom I could help or who could help me.

That track record helped me to recognize that I could not have faked it for this long and in so many areas. While I don't know that I am completely over the impostor syndrome, I erased most of it by accepting that evidence over time. In my interviews with achievers, many of them report a similar path of building confidence on a standard of excellent performance. The impostor syndrome instills a fear of failure that achievers overcome by putting in the extra hours of work and study to make sure they are the best of the best.

That is exactly the mind-set and pattern of thoughts and behaviors you'll want to model in order to join this elite group.

Make excellence your standard of performance. No one builds a statue in the park for being the most average or mediocre performer. There are no rewards for spending the most time surfing the net or watching TV. Take full responsibility for your actions and results. Realize that you are perfectly programmed to get the results you are getting. If you want to improve the results, you must improve your programming.

Step 1 is to decide you want to be successful. Most people never consider it, but you can. Once you have decided to become successful, begin to read and study the patterns of thought and behaviors of successful people.

AUTOMATIC BEHAVIOR PATTERNS

Studies show that we spend, on average, 88 percent of our day in automatic behavior patterns. These are the actions we take throughout each day that we don't even think about. Driving, brushing our teeth, tying our shoes, watching TV are all behaviors that we engage in each day in a light trance state where our mind is thinking on a conscious level of something while our subconscious mind executes the behavior pattern. Our goal is to make the thought and behavior patterns of successful people as automatic as driving a car.

These psychographic groups help us understand the power of programming. It's interesting that when you look at the strugglers or belongers there is usually a multigenerational dynamic going on. Rarely would the child of an achiever end up as a struggler.

The family-oriented nature of the belonger keeps that group large and homogenous. When you look at the explorer, you sense a rebellion against conventional programming. The achiever, unless he or she is raised in an achievers' home, doesn't exactly rebel but reprograms himself or herself to become more successful.

Of all of the segments, the achiever is the most connected to the short-term-pain long-term-gain strategy of life. Achievers associate a lot of pain with being unproductive. Notice, I didn't say they associate a lot of pain with lack of work. Most strugglers and belongers work harder and more laborious than the achiever. The achiever values brains over brawn. The difference is that the achiever learns to develop automatic behavior patterns that keep him or her focused on the areas of high results rather than just working. The guy who mows my four-acre lawn works a heck of a lot harder than I do. He's a great guy, patient with my ever-curious children and a dedicated father. He's a classic belonger. He works his rear end off for his family, and he has my total respect.

The achiever is willing to risk opportunity and time to learn the skills and build the foundation of long-term success. There is little risk in mowing lawns, so there is little reward. This is why my lawn guy works sunup to sundown to support his family.

The achiever fashions systems and processes that create income whether he or she works that day or not. The achievers, through investments and automatic businesses, wake up with more money than they went to bed with. Is this easy to do? No. Is it a scary and risky path to take? Yes. But, as Brian Tracy taught many years ago, "If your heart is not in your throat at least once a day, you are not trying hard enough." I never forgot that bit of advice.

Pain and Gain Exercise

Determining which of the segments of society you are in will help you know how to motivate yourself. When you are aware of what pains and what pleases you, you can associate pain with the short-term gain and pleasure with the long-term gain.

1. The Struggler
2. The Socially Conscious
3. The Belonger
4. The Explorer
5. The Emulator
6. The Achiever

Reread the descriptions above of the pain and gain of the group you inhabit. How could you use the knowledge of yourself to get moving in the right direction?

PAIN AND GAIN EXERCISE

1. Determining which of the segments of society you are in will help you know how to motivate yourself.

    The Struggler
    The Socially Conscious
    The Belonger
    The Explorer
    The Emulator
    The Achiever

2. Which group best describes you?

3. Is it the group you want to be in?

4. What group would you like to aspire to?

5. What steps do you need to take to begin to move there?

6. What gain/pain associations are holding you back?

7. How can you change them to move you forward?

Chapter Twelve

THE CONTROL FACTOR

There is a direct correlation between your level of happiness and the level of control you think you have in your life.

S tudies show that much of your happiness is in direct proportion to the control you have in your life. The more you think you are in control of your life and its direction, the happier and more content you will be.

When I was young, the tension in my house was so thick my dad used to say, "You could cut it with a knife." I joined the karate school as an escape. As a young person, of course, I had very little control over my life. I was at the mercy of my parents and almost everyone else in authority or bigger than me. The karate school gave me a way to gain control, power, and respect.

Even though the classes were sometimes brutal, I knew that if I followed instructions and endured the pain, I would earn the respect that comes from advancing in the belt ranks. As you advance in rank, your position within the school rises with the level of respect for higher belts. With each belt came more control for me. I went from being intimidated and powerless at home to being accorded respect at the karate school. I was gaining control of my life. That is the beauty of how the martial arts can help you to redefine yourself.

REDEFINING YOURSELF

As I entered adulthood, I was hired to teach classes for $5 per class. At the same time, I had a day job as a bus boy clearing tables, where my experience was, "Graden! Clear off table 6!" At night in the karate school, it was, "Mr. Graden. Would you please have a talk with Joey? He's getting into trouble at school. He looks up to you so much . . ."

Which do you think appealed to me? As a martial artist, I was gaining control of my life, and it was wonderful. The martial arts gave me a sense of identity and significance.

In psychology, the principle of control in your life is referred to as "locus of control," and it's generally agreed that an external locus of control tends to be negative. If you think your life is controlled by debt, your job, a bad relationship, or the behavior of others, this is an external locus of control; and it creates tremendous stress. It feels as though you are a boat without a rudder, being blown by the winds of misfortune.

Over time, this can develop into depression, insomnia, and an overall feeling of resentment and resignation about your situation. Much stress, frustration, and anxiety, along with the physical ills they create, are the results of feeling out of control in some important area of life.

GAINING CONTROL

An internal locus of control is the feeling that you are in charge of your life. Replacing an external locus of control with an internal locus of control starts with your own patterns of thought. Really, your patterns of thought and behavior are all that you can control. How you frame and reframe situations is your choice and determines how you feel and act.

Destroying self-doubt and building self-control begins with gaining control of your patterns of thought. You have to accept that no one can make you feel bad or act in a certain way without your consent. Only you can control your thoughts and actions. You decide how to think. It takes practice, but this single strategy is critical.

Certainly, taking responsibility for how you think is not always easy. Going through my divorce was heart wrenching. It's an awful feeling, and I certainly didn't choose to feel that way. The range of emotions certainly included anger, but I recognized that only I could control how I acted. Anger and heartache are not conscious thought patterns, so it's not always easy to make them disappear; but I was in total control of how I acted in that state. Emotions have a purpose and a message. Being angry and hurt does not mean you have to act out on that anger and pain. Rather than act out on anger, I focused on building a new business and new life.

I had to move on with my life and allow my ex-wife to do the same. It was not always easy, but it could have been a lot worse had we allowed the natural pain and anger that typically comes with a divorce to control our actions. Neither one of us fell into the trap of wanting to exert punishment on the other for the pain we were both enduring. We realized that the stress of the lawsuits and a horrific car accident pushed us apart rather than together. Once we divorced, we decided to focus on our children rather than each other. As a result, we are better friends now than in the final years of our marriage.

I also avoided the common divorce rebound strategy that could have compounded my stress. Instead, using much of what I'm sharing in this book, I reworked my patterns of thought and behavior regarding dating and approaching women. I created a new strategy to meet new women in order to make sure I was not taking the first one to come along. It worked beautifully; and after about eight months of fun and dating, I zeroed in on a very special lady indeed.

While the ability to gain control of your life starts with controlling your patterns of thought, it's your ability to take decisive action that will have the most direct impact. Sometimes it's better to go through the short-term pain of ending a relationship for the long-term gain of moving on with your life. Again, we come back to the strategy of short-term pain for long-term gain. Somewhere I heard this referred to as "eating your crust first." It's better to eat the crust first so you can enjoy the rest of the slice.

CONTROL EXERCISE

1. List areas in your life over which you think you have little control and the areas you think you have control over.

   In Control

   _____

   _____

   Out of Control

   _____

   _____

2. Why do you feel you have little control in these areas? Are these valid reasons, or are you mired in a comfort zone?

   _____

   _____

3. What can you do, starting right now, to gain control in those areas or eliminate them from your life? (Eat your crust first.)

   _____

   _____

   _____

Chapter Thirteen

STUDENTS AND THE IMPOSTOR SYNDROME

Perfectionism is a classic impostor syndrome symptom.

The impostor syndrome may be more prevalent for students possibly because they are constantly reviewed, graded, and critiqued on a regular basis. The results of these evaluations can have a huge impact on their lives and future, so there is a constant pressure to perform and succeed.

Evaluations and the accompanying stress increase as the student with the impostor syndrome moves into higher education. For instance, students in graduate programs have to demonstrate and/or write about theory and practical applications in their major. A failure at any point could result in their progress toward a career goal screeching to an abrupt halt.

Even after they graduate and move into their new field, it is often a licensed profession with more examinations and qualifications for various licenses and regulations. Again, all of these potential reviews are stress-inducing crossroads where everything could end with a single failure.

Students with the impostor syndrome tend to be perfectionists because they are terrified of failing and being found out as an intellectual fraud. (Perfectionists are usually not fun people to be around.) School and testing are results oriented. They are very black and white as answers are either right or wrong. The real world is painted in various shades of gray where there are often many answers to a challenge.

Because of my own impostor syndrome tendencies, I enjoyed the martial arts because the road to success was clearly laid out. If I did the techniques with as near-perfect form as possible, I couldn't fail.

However, I began to see the world in the black and white of whether something was "correct" or "flawed." As a result, I enjoyed pointing out the flaws in various aspects of life, including my friends. Finally, one of them had enough and told me I was hypercritical.

That viewpoint, combined with maturity and experience, helped me begin to see the world in varying shades of gray and, in time, as a Technicolor vista.

When your happiness and sense of well-being are tied to your creating a perfect world or conducting yourself in a perfect manner, you are electing to have neither happiness nor well-being. Striving for perfection is a classic case of setting yourself up for failure. No one is perfect, not even us.

Chapter Fourteen

FAKE IT UNTIL YOU MAKE IT

My time machine for success.

In 1987, I was hired by Allstate Insurance to present a motivational seminar for their sales team. One of their executives had seen me speak on TV and thought I could help his team. This was my first motivational speech.

It's kind of ironic because I was dead broke at the time and would be "motivating" a group of salesmen earning six-figure incomes. But in the spirit of "fake it until you make it," I created a twenty-minute presentation, mixing martial arts and inspiration.

For instance, I had one of my students attack me then I took away his balance by sweeping him to the floor. Next, I turned to the audience to describe the importance of balance in life. I thought I was way out of my league, but they loved it. Allstate doubled my pay to $1,000 and booked six more seminars.

More than the money, the confidence I gained from the experience was life changing. Had I not been willing to fake it, I would have had no chance to make it.

MY TIME MACHINE

As part of the compensation for the speech, Allstate booked me in a room at the downtown Hilton in St. Petersburg, Florida. That was the nicest hotel I'd ever been in at the time. Though I lived just two miles away, I opted to spend the night at the Hilton. That evening I sat in the lounge, creating list after list of new goals for myself.

The response to the seminar was so positive that it catapulted my confidence to new levels, and I made goals with a new sense of daring and ambition. This was a major emotional threshold in my life. Had I sat down a couple of days earlier to make a list of goals, they would have been far less ambitious than the list I made that night in the Hilton.

While you may not yet have had an experience such as speaking for a group of executives, what would be the equivalent in your life? Is there a short-term goal or accomplishment that would give you the same confidence boost? Here is a little technique that will help you to get that confidence boost right now.

I want you to name the goal or if the goal is really large, name the first step and then repeat this process for each step toward accomplishing that goal.

For instance, if you want to change careers, you may want to start with taking a class or a seminar in the field you want to transition to.

Second would be to get whatever license or certification may be required. The third step might be to make the transition. Write these steps down or fix them in your mind right now.

After reading this chapter, close your eyes and project your mind forward and imagine that you have accomplished that first step. What does that feel like? See yourself accomplishing your goal. Listen to the congratulations from your friends and family. I want you to feel it, see it, hear it, taste it, and smell the sweet aroma of success. Drink it all in for a moment before moving on to the next step and the next step until you have accomplished your goal.

How does that feel? Pretty good, I bet. This projection technique is a powerful way to motivate yourself and stimulate your subconscious mind. It attracts you to the activities required to accomplish your goal.

This method works best when you are alone for part of a day and surrounded by an environment of wealth. The best place for me to do my goal setting is in a nice hotel. When I did this that first night in the Hilton, just being around wealthier people made me feel rich. Mind you, at the time, if you had $100 in the bank, you were richer than me; so it didn't take much, but I think you get the idea.

The difference the surroundings made in my attitude convinced me to go to a luxury hotel each year to do my goal setting. I've done this now in Dubai, London, Paris, Hawaii, Germany, Aspen, Grand Cayman, and other fabulous locations; and you can too.

Spend at least one day in a five-star hotel, reviewing the year and planning for the next. Even if you don't book a room at the hotel, you can do this in the lobby or lounge. The strategy is to surround yourself with privilege and an atmosphere of wealth to help you formulate your goals for the new year.

Here some simple annual goals to set:

1. Improve your net worth by 10 percent.
2. Increase personal income by 20 percent.
3. Pay off all debt other than your mortgage.
4. Pay off your mortgage (I've never had a mortgage last more than three years).

THE OPEN HOUSE TECHNIQUE

Another enjoyable goal-projection technique is one of my favorites. On weekends, realtors open houses to visitors. Go visit million-dollar homes. I did this for years. I'd walk in and pretend this was my house. I'd take a deep breath and inhale the smell of a millionaire's home. I'd imagine I was coming home from work and heading for the hot tub with a cool drink to relax and enjoy my surroundings.

Rich, glossy magazines like *The Robb Report* are also ways you can visit fabulous homes without having to leave your own.

If you've never experienced wealth or set a goal and accomplished it, then it may be difficult to imagine yourself getting there. The purpose of these goal-projection exercises is to stimulate your subconscious mind to pull you in the direction that you want to go. Immersing yourself in an atmosphere of wealth creates an internal sensation that you are already there.

Remember, the subconscious doesn't know the difference between what is real and what is imagined. This is a step toward creating a new reality for yourself.

Time Machine Exercise

1. Imagine it is two years from now. What would your life be like for you to be satisfied with the past two years?

2. Are you still working at the same job? Why?

3. What is your income? Why?

4. What is your debt level?

5. What new skills have you developed?

6. Are you in the same relationship? Why?

Chapter Fifteen

FIRE! READY! AIM!

How to avoid the trap of analysis paralysis.

A nalysis paralysis is a symptom of self-doubt. You have analysis paralysis when you know an idea or a goal that will improve your life, but self-doubt causes you to hesitate initiating the steps toward the goal. Rather than attacking, you spend an inordinate amount of time analyzing and studying.

This hesitation shows itself in different ways. For instance, someone takes a sales course after sales course as a way of avoiding going out and actually making a sale. The character Zonker Harris in the comic strip Doonesbury was a professional student who remained in college for as long as possible to avoid going out into the real world.

Others never take the first step because they are entrenched in their comfort zone and would rather avoid trying something new than to try something new and fail or fall short.

THE COMFORT ZONE OF LOW PERFORMANCE

This fear of failure is the single biggest affliction in society. If you look at anyone in a low-paying, dead-end job or who stays in an unhealthy relationship, you are seeing a person who fears failure and prefers to stay in a comfort zone. "The known devil is better than the unknown devil" is their mind-set and strategy for living. Rather than improving his or her skills to get a better job or to walk away from a bad relationship, he or she stays because of fear that things will only get worse. This is another example of short-term gain for long-term pain.

These people complain about their situation but never take the action to improve it. They say things like, "It's too late for me . . ." or "What am I going to do? I'm forty-six years old!" and "He's a friend. He doesn't have the money to give me a raise . . ." They come up with all kinds of excuses to justify their lack of action. The truth is, as Mark Twain said, "You can have a thousand good excuses but not one good reason."

Fire! Ready! Aim!

"Fire, ready, aim" is a great strategy that has worked for me for years. It is meant to kick-start your progress. It's designed to create a sense of urgency from idea to implementation.

The traditional process of "ready, aim, fire" is a process of preparation (ready), specific direction (aim), and then implementation (fire). That makes sense and is the safe way to go. The problem for me with this strategy is that it's easy to get stuck in the ready and aim segments. As I described above, many people seem to spend their entire adult lives "getting ready."

Here is the reality: Any goal worth reaching will not be achieved without encountering speed bumps along the way. You can prepare as much as you like; but once you pull the trigger, you will get feedback, sometimes negative, that helps you stay on course. The sooner you get feedback, the more quickly you can make your course adjustments. Preparation doesn't give you real-time feedback. It gives you only theories of what may happen. Theories don't move you forward. Action does.

"Fire, ready, aim" reverses the traditional process to jump-start your progress and the feedback process. The idea is to "make the mess and clean it up later." Get on with it. Go! Go! GO! Pull the trigger on the project first and make the adjustments as you go. Develop a sense of urgency in everything you do.

There is an obvious caution regarding this strategy. If your goal is to become an airline pilot or considering a financial investment, "fly, ready, aim" would not be a smart strategy. There are plenty of projects and goals where it makes sense to get the skills required to not kill yourself or lose your fortune. But in my experience, the vast majority of projects and goals that people set would be far more easily accomplished by pulling the trigger before getting caught in analysis paralysis.

Pulling the trigger may well be taking a course of study, but not avoiding the actual activity with endless training programs. I don't want to diminish the importance of self-education. I attribute my success to what I've learned through reading books like this, listening to audio programs, and attending courses.

The Three Times Rule

Here is a good rule: Spend three times as much time doing as you spend learning. If you spend three days in a course, spend the next nine days doing what you learned.

Writing My First Book

In 1993, I began to write my first book, *Black Belt Management*. I only had a GED for high school and had never excelled at writing, nor did I particularly enjoy the process as I do now. Writing that book was hard work. From the time I had the idea to the time the book was printed was nine months. Fortunately, the book sold so well I was able to pay my house off within two years. Had I, like so many others, simply had an idea for a book or spent those nine months researching how to write a book, I doubt that would ever have happened.

I was able to parlay the success of the book into creating the martial arts industry's first professional trade association and trade journal.

OVER $30 MILLION

In late 1993, I was speaking at a small convention for martial arts school owners in Las Vegas. The host of the event, Larry Doke, and his partner Rick Bell approached me at the beginning of the event. They presented me with a set of business cards that read, John Graden-President, National Association of Professional Martial Artists. Larry said, "John. You're the only person who can do this."

That vote of confidence was all I needed. I launched the association by sending out seven hundred sample packages to martial arts school owners in December 1993. As a member, each school would get a physical package from me each month with a camera-ready ad they could use, audio and video seminars, and other items to help them grow their school.

That generated over $30 million over the next decade and made me a millionaire. I had no idea what a professional association was, nor had I ever published a magazine before. I didn't let that slow me down. I attacked. Fire, ready, aim.

I didn't have an office or staff in place; but rather than wait until everything was in place, I pulled the trigger. During the next thirty days, 125 schools joined at $99 per month. At its peak, the association had over two thousand schools paying $99 every month. My magazine had a circulation of over twenty-five thousand, and my convention was the largest in the industry.

Had I really sat down and analyzed it, I would have never launched. But I followed the fire-ready-aim rule! The magazine's first issue almost broke me. I never ran the numbers on it but knew in my heart the industry needed a quality journal and that advertisers would step up to support it, and they did. I had no formal training in any area of running these businesses, but I pulled the trigger on them so fast I never sat down to let self-doubt talk me out of them.

Here's another example. I became a certified hypnotist in November 2006. Within thirty days, I started writing a book that profiled the top hypnotists here and in the United Kingdom. That immediately put me in contact with the best of the best. By interviewing each of them on how they built their practices and created wealth in this unusual profession, I became friends with the top hypnotists in the world. One of them, Dr. Will Horton, who is also a black belt, offered to coauthor a leadership book with me that would combine the mental skills of the martial arts with the power of hypnosis.

Part of my strategy in writing the book was to find out how I could best integrate hypnosis into my professional life. I didn't want to depend on one-on-one sessions. As much as I enjoy them, it's trading time for money; and that's a slow road to wealth. I discovered that hypnosis gave me a unique element that, combined with my martial arts background and success in business, would provide me with the perfect platform to expand my professional speaking career.

Once I realized that, I started playing with titles for seminars and books. As I mentioned elsewhere, at two thirty in the morning, the title for the book you're reading hit me. Before drifting off to sleep, I made a list of what I thought would go into the table of contents, which helped me formulate the content.

The next morning I attacked the project and wrote two chapters and committed to a chapter a day until it was done. *Black Belt Management* took nine months to write; the book you are reading took four weeks. From being certified in hypnosis to writing the hypnosis book until completing this book has been just under three months. That is "fire, ready, aim" in action. Attack! Attack! Attack!

PROGRESS NOT PERFECTION

A key mind-set to making this strategy work is to seek progress, not perfection. Though I've used that mind-set for years, Dan Sullivan of the Strategic Coach Program was the first person I've heard describe it as, "progress not perfection." Like a shark, you want to keep moving forward toward improving your life and achieving your goal.

Measure your success on the progress you've made. You will have setbacks and failures, but you will still be closer to your goal of improving your life than if you hadn't done anything.

Break down your big goals into smaller, more accessible goals. That's why we use the belt system in the martial arts. The goal for all of my students is black belt. While I have accelerated courses that can get you to black belt in as little as six months, it takes most students three to five years of classes. That is a long time, so we break up that time frame with short-term goals represented by belt colors.

In most schools, the darker the belt, the closer to black belt you get. So in my school, you start with white belt. The white represents knowing nothing or very little about martial arts.

Within six weeks, you earn your gold belt; and then in eight- to twelve-week increments, you go to orange, green, blue, red, fourth degree brown, third degree brown, second degree brown, first degree brown, and finally black.

Each belt is earned through an examination process. With each belt earned, the students feel a sense of progress. These act as minivictories that motivate them to continue classes. It is important for student retention that every eligible student takes his or her exams. We knew from tracking our statistics that students who did not take exams were our highest dropout risks. Progress creates motivation. "Fire, ready, aim" creates progress, which in turn creates momentum and motivation.

To be clear, "fire, ready, aim" can create some challenges and setbacks that could have been avoided with more preparation, but in my experience—and this book is only my perspective on these things—the results far outweigh the risks.

Despite what all of the business books suggest, I've never written a business plan nor have I ever used one. I've never written a marketing plan either. For small businesses like mine, I don't see the need to outline and prepare for every contingency. For large businesses, I can see how having plans can help keep everyone's ladder on the same wall. But I would rather spend that time attacking my next project.

Yes, "fire, ready, aim" can create some problems of its own that you may avoid with more planning, but the key word is "may." You might encounter the same problem with planning. Who knows? Who cares? Just get on with it. I believe that if you pull the trigger you will get the feedback you need from the market, rather than a theory.

"FIRE, READY, AIM!" EXERCISE

1. What projects or ideas have you been stalling on and why?

2. What would be the rewards of pulling the trigger?

3. What is the first step toward pulling the trigger?

4. *What would be the risks?

5. What's stopping you now?

Chapter Sixteen

No Middle Ground

The quality of your decisions determines the quality of your life.

In this chapter lies the real opportunity to change your life. This key strategy is to always seek a way to turn a negative into a positive.

This is what I mean by changing your thinking. When I get frustrated, upset, or preoccupied with a negative situation, I've learned to replace that thought with positive, strategic thinking about what my next step is toward my goals. What is before me that will move me toward my goals? This thought replaces the negative thoughts that attempt to pull me down as I run toward my goals.

You will often find that the negative thoughts are about events or situations that have already happened. They are "done deals," and nothing can be done about them. They are bells that can't be unrung.

Their negative impact on your life is compounded with every minute of thought you give them. It is compounded because, as you are wasting life being preoccupied with the negative, you cannot occupy your mind with the goal-oriented, positive, strategic thinking you need to ultimately succeed.

Also, to the degree you spend time dwelling on these negative thoughts and experiences, you are allowing them to define you. You never want to let the negative events in your life define your life.

Your School of Life

Consider what has happened in your life in the past as your school of life. You learn from it. You don't stay mired in it.

We've all had bad things happened to us, and we've all done things we wish we hadn't. The old saying is, "A clear conscience is a sign of a bad memory."

When you refuse to dwell on a problem, it begins to lose its effect on you. When you put off a negative thought, you reduce the level of control it has on you. Conversely, when you think about it all the time, it keeps you completely preoccupied and uses so much of your mental capacity and energy that you cannot do much of anything else. You do not have time to spend on building success when you waste time on negative thinking.

Your Ledger of Success

Imagine that you have a one-page "success ledger." Your goals are written across the top of the paper. Down the center of the page is a vertical line. On the left side, the heading is "Takes Me Closer to My Goals." On the right side is, "Takes Me Further from My Goals." Every decision you make is listed on one side or the other. If every fifteen minutes, you were to write down your thoughts, decisions, and the resulting actions, which side would fill up faster?

There is no middle ground.

Every minute spent preoccupied with negative thinking is a minute delayed in moving toward your goal. Any decision that does not directly move you toward your goals has the effect of delaying its achievement; hence, it is moving you farther away. Make sure your decisions take you closer to your goals.

The quality of your decisions determines the quality of your life. Success is not easy. It comes from intense focus and concentration on what takes you closer to your goals. Most of all, success comes from taking full responsibility for achieving your goals, from your smallest thoughts to your largest decisions.

No excuses, no complaining, no blaming. Just hard, focused work toward your goal. You deserve it, just as I deserve it. It does not matter if you don't know anyone else who has done it yet in your circle of family and friends. Only you can make it happen, and I know you can.

Chapter Seventeen

WHAT HAPPENED TO
YOU DOESN'T DEFINE YOU

What matters is how you deal with it.

For me, with the exception of the birth of my second son, Christopher, 2001 to 2008 was a nightmare of lawsuits, divorce, loss, and a terrible car accident. How I chose to frame these events was entirely up to me. I could have given up and crawled into a corner somewhere, but I didn't.

People were surprised at my positive attitude about losing everything. My response was, "What's the alternative?" While I can't control what other people do, I can control how I choose to deal with what is happening. The way I chose to frame those events was that losing everything is a fascinating process.

I'm not saying I didn't have stress. No way. Pepto Bismol was always within arm's reach. Let me tell you, this was a painful experience. However, I refused to allow those events to define me, any more than I would allow my successes to define me. All that matters is how I respond. All I can control is my pattern of thought and behavior.

(Incidentally, I found it interesting how people respond when you go from being the top guy to having nearly all of your resources taken from you. I was amazed that the friends and family members whom I would have bet money would try to help out completely abandoned me, while people I hardly knew stepped up big time. Either way, it was not in my control.)

THE KARATE JOCK

For the first twenty years of my training, the martial arts defined who I was. I used the martial arts to transform myself from chubby teenager to athletic "karate jock." Martial arts were virtually all I talked about. All my friends were martial artists. Even if I went to a volleyball tournament, it was usually with a bunch of black belts.

For years, being a champion black belt on TV was my identity. It wasn't until I launched the National Association of Professional Martial Artists (NAPMA) in 1993 that I began to realize that, while martial arts helped me to reinvent my own identity, the job was only half done. I had to reintegrate my martial arts with my inner self so that martial arts became an expression of who I was, not the entire definition.

If you are allowing your success or lack of it to be your identity, then you're hiding your real self. A good example are film stars who choose not to live in Hollywood because they view their stardom as an extension of who they are, instead of the definition of their identity.

Sandra Bullock lives in Texas, and it's pretty clear when you see her in interviews that she views acting as a high-paying job she enjoys, but that there is also much more to her than just acting. In contrast, Jack Nicholson is iconic in his identity as a film star. Being a movie star is his identity.

By the same token, when something bad happens to you or you do something you wish you hadn't, be careful not to let that define you either. This is not always easy, but it's critically important.

MENTAL PRISON

Often when something bad happens or someone does something bad to you, it creates a mental prison that confines your self-image and potential for growth.

When the action against you is really horrendous, such as molestation or abuse, the prison so tightly confines you that your self-image may be built around this event for the rest of your life.

Here's the reality. You did nothing to deserve what happened to you; and while you are obsessing with the negatives associated with the event—and they can be horrible—the person who committed the act is doing laundry. You are not on their mind, yet they are on your mind for as long as you allow them to be.

If I allowed myself, it would be easy to become mired in the mud of self-pity and absorb myself in negative thoughts and behaviors toward the man who sued me to try to control me. What I've realized is that, like all of us, the person who wrongs you is a product of his own programming. Once I understood that, it was easier to forgive him.

Forgiving him does not condone what he did, nor does it make it right. I think what he did is sick. He is what my mother calls "a little man." But I refuse to allow what he did to me to keep me in the prison of a negative mind.

What is the alternative? While I obsess over his attacks on me, he goes and plays a round of golf. If I hold on to the negative effects of his attacks, it's as though I give him permission to compound the effects into all areas of my life. Well, permission is not granted.

A better example of turning a negative into a positive is the amazing way John Walsh turned the brutal murder of his five-year-old son Adam into a career of catching criminals on *America's Most Wanted*. It's hard to fathom the pain he must have felt losing his little boy. Yet rather than staying stuck in that horrible event, he moved his life forward in a positive manner. I have no doubt he is making his son very proud of his daddy.

What happened to you, good and bad, is not you. What defines you more accurately is how you deal with it.

Chapter Eighteen

HOW TO ALIGN WITH YOUR GOALS

Eliminating the obstacles to your aspirations.

This is a great technique taught to me by my friend Dr. Will Horton. He calls this the logical levels technique. It is a technique that I will walk you through on the audio segments in the readers' section of TheImpostorSyndrome.com. When you listen to it, you can engage your imagination to embrace these ideas. But for right now, here is how the logical levels technique works.

Pick one of your most important goals. Imagine that on the floor in front of you is a six-step staircase to your goal. Each step represents a required level in reaching your goal.

When you have all six levels in line, your life is congruent with your goal. As you will see, if any level is not aligned, your life is incongruent with your goal, which creates conflict. Any incongruence creates obstacles for moving toward your goal.

LEVEL 1: YOUR ENVIRONMENT

Is your current environment conducive to reaching your goal?

If you have to study, do you have an environment to do so? Do you have the books, CDs, manuals you need? If not, how can you get them? Who is your teacher? If you are trying to lose weight, stop smoking or drinking, have you eliminated those substances from your environment?

Are the people in your life supportive of your goal? Do they encourage you or discourage you from growing? If they are discouraging, is there a way to get them to allow you the space to grow? Is there a way to get away from them? Do you need to change your circle of friends?

Do you need to make changes to your environment? Can you create an environment that is supportive and conducive to your achieving this goal? If so, what changes do you need to make? How will you make them?

When you have either determined that your environment is conducive to reaching your goal or you have figured out what steps you have to take to get there, move to the next level.

LEVEL 2: YOUR BEHAVIOR

What behaviors do you need each day, and are you willing to do them?

Are your patterns of behavior supporting your goal? As described earlier in this book, your patterns of thought and behavior define your life. Are you behaving in a manner that is congruent with your goal? If study is required, are you studying? If applying a certain skill is required, are you applying or refining the skill? If a certain behavior pattern such as being drink, smoke, or drug free is required, are you adhering to that pattern? Are you doing what you need to do each day in order to reach your goal? If not, why not?

As I mentioned earlier, I had the idea for this book exactly fifteen days ago at the time of this writing. The title came to me on Monday, February 12. I set a goal to write at least one chapter per day in order to have the book completed by the end of the month. To accomplish this goal, I instantly associated massive pain with not writing.

If I had any free time, I had to be in front of my Mac writing. Had I just "had an idea for a book" and left it at that, the book would have never been written. I then spent another month reworking, rewriting, and getting peer reviews to make sure the book didn't read like it had been written in thirty days. The point is that I attacked the project within minutes of having the idea.

WHAT SEPARATES THE BEST OF US FROM THE REST OF US

The world is full of great ideas; it's taking action and making an idea a reality that separates the best of us from the rest of us.

As a side note, my first karate class was on February 12, 1974; I got married on February 12, 2000; and I had the idea for this book on February 12, 2007. I don't know what that means, but I think it's interesting. At the least, every February 12, I am ready for a great idea!

Are you rationalizing poor behaviors? As I mentioned earlier, sometimes we get caught in an analysis paralysis where we spend more time thinking than doing. This level is all about what you are doing, not thinking or planning. This is not about what you will do once you have reached your goal. This is about doing the behaviors necessary right now to move you toward your goal.

Sometimes clients will confuse this with the rationalization, "I'll do that once I get this done." I'll start exercising when I lose weight. I'll stop smoking when I get in better shape. I'll approach a woman after I've lost ten pounds. I'll start studying to get a new job after I get a raise at this one. These are examples of stall tactics to delay taking responsibility for your actions.

That is not acceptable behavior for a winner. You are too smart to let your mind play those kinds of tricks on you. Let the rest of the people in the world deceive themselves, not you.

Once you have defined the behaviors and committed to doing them, you can move to the next square. If you are not willing to commit to doing them, your goal stops here.

LEVEL 3: YOUR CAPABILITIES

Do you have the capabilities required to reach your goal? In order to reach your goal, you may have to develop some new techniques, strategies, mind-sets, or skills.

You may already have all that you need to move forward, or there may be something that you need to learn or adapt into your life. For instance, a friend of mine wants to become a court reporter. She has to learn how to use a stenowriter and the fascinating, but challenging, methods of phonetic stenographer skills. Once she learns the theory for the machine, she has to increase accuracy and speed to 240 words per minute. She spends a few hours per night working on her lessons through a home study course.

Maybe the new capability you need is not as easily definable as a new career but instead requires a new mind-set or strategy.

For instance, if losing weight is your goal, you'll want to adapt new strategies for eating as we explored in the chapter on "Setting New Strategies." If getting out of debt is your goal, then you will want to create a mind-set that spending money, especially on interest, is very painful. Associate massive pain with spending money. Associate massive pleasure with having money in the bank and a shrinking debt load.

Once you have defined the capabilities and determined that you have them or have outlined a method of obtaining them, you can move to the next level.

LEVEL 4: YOUR BELIEF

Do your beliefs support this goal? What beliefs do you need in order to make this happen?

If you believe that money is the root of all evil, then setting a goal of saving $100,000 may be incongruent with your belief. If it is your belief that in order to be attractive you must be wealthy, drive a cool car, or be in perfect shape, then setting a goal of meeting someone special may be inhibited if you don't have these attributes. If you believe that there are no opportunities for someone who has not finished high school, then your belief is going to limit your possibilities if you didn't graduate.

Remember the Santa Claus example from the chapter "Creating Healthy Beliefs"? Not only will your belief systems change over time, but you can also accelerate the change process and target specific beliefs that you know are holding you back.

The key to quickly changing a belief is to associate massive pain with the old belief and associate massive pleasure with the new belief. Think about how that old belief has held you back and stagnated your potential. See all the missed opportunities and grief this belief caused you. Feel the pain this belief has caused you and others. Does that create a frustrated feeling within you? Good! Amplify that feeling.

Imagine if you had this healthier new belief ten years ago. What would your life be like? See the huge gap between where you could be and where you are. This belief caused that gap. That gap represents pain. The pain is the pain of not having the life that is your God-given right.

Now, reframe that belief into one that motivates you and pulls you in the direction you want to go. Here are some examples of how you can reframe old beliefs into new ones:

MONEY BELIEF REFRAME

Money is a tool that you can use for good. You can help more people when you have more money. Abraham Lincoln said, "We cannot help the poor by becoming one of them." You can help your family when you have more money. You will sleep better at night knowing you have emergency funds when something goes awry. Money is a result of service to other people.

Money does not care what you do with it. It is neutral. You can do as much good as you possibly can with money when, and only when, you have money. You will not be able to help people with money if you don't have any. I've been rich and I've been poor; and believe me, rich is much better simply because the stress of paying bills is out of your life.

ATTRACTION BELIEF REFRAME

Excuse me for going a little long on this subject. This reframe was very powerful for me. It started with the realization that attraction is not an intellectual choice or decision. We see too many average men with beautiful women and handsome men with average women to support that belief.

The truth is that a good person looks for qualities, not things. As we learned in chapter 11, "You Are Not Alone," belongers focus more on qualities, whereas emulators in particular focus on material things.

How much money does the person make? What kind of car does he drive? What kind of job does she have? Those are examples of focusing on things rather than qualities.

Success certainly has attractive qualities about it. However, I don't want someone attracted to me because I have a big house with a tennis court. I want someone who finds my accomplishments to be an extension of the qualities of who I am as a person.

Ambition is a quality. Taking good care of yourself is a quality. Having a sense of humor is an important quality. A healthy, resilient optimism is a good quality. An empathetic nature is a good quality. Being a good conversationalist is a good quality. Qualities reflect who you are as a person and also affect the emotional experience a person will have with you.

When you are with someone who reaches places within you that maybe you didn't even know existed, you will find massive attraction. I want her to say, "I've never met anyone like you before," not "I've never met anyone with a car like yours before."

When you believe that you must have things in order to attract someone, the message is that you are inadequate without those things. That is the impostor syndrome in action.

After I was divorced, I made some conscious decisions regarding being single at forty-five. After a relationship breakup in the past, my impostor syndrome tendencies would talk my way out of approaching someone attractive. This would result in extended periods of not dating until someone came along that I liked enough to make my girlfriend. I call that the "girlfriend by default." You kind of fall into meeting someone without much effort.

My self-doubt held me back from pursuing attractive women I didn't know. An example was my ex-wife Lynette. She is a wonderful woman and an amazing mother. I was always very proud to have her as my wife. But I didn't approach her. Her girlfriend grabbed her and said, "There is the man for you," and pulled her right over to me. We were together for nine years and married for seven.

Regrettably, the marriage was not able to survive the lawsuits and a horrific car accident she suffered while driving our boys and her mom. She and her mom had to be cut out of the car and flown by helicopter to the hospital. All this happened with our kids, who were just age four and two at the time, sitting in the backseat, hysterical. Things were never the same after that, but we had an amicable divorce and are good friends today.

After the divorce, though, I knew that meeting women was an area of my life that I wanted to gain more control over. I determined that dating was going to be different, and it was. I promised myself that no matter how great a girl was, I would not commit to anyone for at least six months. I didn't want to rebound.

Next, I started to study material relating to the subconscious mind and the nature of attraction. Guys, think about this: Who taught (programmed) you about dating? Probably your mom. Well, I'm sure it's not the case with many people, but I was born to two parents on their third marriage. That's not exactly the track record you want to get relationship advice from.

While my parents did the best they could, I knew I had to reprogram my mind on approaching and dating women. I began to study some fascinating material that I wish I had been exposed to twenty-five years ago. You can find those resources on TheImpostorSyndrome.com. If you are single and, like most of us, experience some approach anxiety, stop reading right now and go check this material out.

I dated two to four women per week for months until I finally settled on one great girl. The change in my belief regarding approaching women made a huge difference in my life.

EDUCATION BELIEF REFRAME

Formal education is great but not necessary to succeed. There are too many examples of people who have done extraordinarily well by learning from their real-life experience rather than an ivory tower theory. Your author is one of them.

Far more impressive is the success of Virgin Records founder Sir Richard Branson, who dropped out of school at age sixteen and went on to become a billionaire. I have had MBAs working for me and college-educated personal assistants who, while in their thirties, were happy to get $10 per hour running my errands.

Do you believe you deserve the rewards this goal will bring you? If no one in your family had ever earned a six-figure income, had healthy relationships, led a healthy life, then it may be hard for you to believe that achieving any of these or your own goals is possible. It's important to understand that your ceiling of potential is not determined by anyone but you. To use a corny phrase, "If you can believe it, you can achieve it." History is full of people overcoming incredible odds, including self-doubt, to achieve remarkable accomplishments. You will be one of them.

When your belief systems are aligned with your goal, you may move to the next level.

LEVEL 5: IDENTITY LEVEL

Does your identity match that of the new version of you that will reach this goal? In chapter 5, "The Conversation of a Lifetime," we determined that much of our inner dialogue may be with younger versions of ourselves. This helps us to understand how such conversations can create massive self-doubt and negative patterns of behavior.

Imagine what it would feel like to have already accomplished your goal. Project your mind into the future, and imagine what it will feel like to be the person who achieved it. Rather than identify with a version of you from the negative past, create an identity of yourself having already accomplished this goal.

The goal of this book is to help you redefine yourself. This goal-projection process is a great way to kick-start that process.

I did this exercise once with a woman during a hypnosis session. She had a goal that would make her a celebrity in her field and generate significant income for her. When we got to this level, I asked her if her identity matched the identity of the person who achieves the goal she wanted. She said, "No." We explored this issue; and it came down to her being afraid that if she made more money than most men, she would not be attractive to them. This was a beautiful blond athlete whose identity did not match that of the person who would reach her goal.

I walked her through a scenario where she was arriving at an event on the arm of a man who was so insecure that he had to make more money than his girlfriend or wife. I had her feel the feelings of being with someone that weak. I had her imagine what her future would be like under the control of someone else's insecurities. I had her associate tremendous pain and disappointment with this scenario.

I then had her walk through the same scenario but with a man who was confident and didn't care how much money she made. He only cared about her and wanted the best for her. I had her imagine what her future would be like with the sincere love and support of someone like this. I had her associate tremendous pleasure and joy with this scenario.

My goal was to help her create the identity that would support her goal. Did it work? It's too early to say; but when she emerged, she said that she had not previously been aware of how money and men played into her identity. That realization alone is a positive step.

When your identity matches that of you on the other side of your goal, you may move to the next level.

Level 6: Spiritual Level

If you believe in a higher power, does that higher power support this goal? With few exceptions, in order for a spiritual belief to be aligned with a goal, the goal has to be honest, ethical, and positive for everyone involved. For instance, if your goal is one of revenge on someone you feel has wronged you, it would be a bit of a stretch ("an eye for an eye" aside) to say that your higher power supports such a negative goal.

Of course, the best revenge is success, and that is usually aligned with a higher power.

I like the logical levels because it really walks you through the various dynamics that affect your ability to accomplish your goals. When these six elements are in place, there is nothing to stop you. If any of them are out of place, you are bound to have a more difficult path toward improving your life.

In a sense, the logical levels work like a reality check for your goal setting. They give dreams and aspirations a concrete foundation and pathway to becoming reality.

LOGICAL LEVELS EXERCISE

What goal would you like to focus on for this exercise?

1. What can you do to make your environment supportive?

2. What behaviors are required to move you toward this goal? Are you executing them?

3. What capabilities do you need to accomplish this goal? What additional capabilities or skills do you need to develop? How will you develop them?

4. Do your current beliefs support this goal? Are there any conflicts with achieving the goal or the rewards?

5. Is achieving this goal congruent with your identity? Why?

6. Is your higher power supportive of this goal?

7. Based upon your answers, what are you going to do?

Chapter Nineteen

TAKE CARE OF YOURSELF FIRST

Being nice and having your goals met don't have to be in conflict.

One of the most important, yet difficult, strategies to implement is taking care of yourself first. Many of us were programmed to sacrifice our needs for those of others. The long-term effect of such a strategy can be to live a life that is dependent upon the happiness of those around us. If our happiness is dependent upon everyone around us being happy, then we've set ourselves up for a life of frustration.

Usually, someone has programmed us to think that it is self-centered to put our needs first. But being confined by someone else's definition of caring for your own needs is a straightjacket. You will never be able to give yourself fully to someone else until your own needs are met.

Think of the word "fulfillment." Is it a bad word? Isn't fulfillment what we all want? But some of us spend our lives trying to fulfill everyone else's life at the expense of our own.

We all know someone, maybe you, who is a very giving person. He or she is sweet and nonconfrontational and will pick up the slack for others. If someone gets mad, he or she apologizes first and fast. He or she makes excuses for other people who treat him or her badly. How authentic is this person? How long can he or she keep up this charade? He or she is playing the role of a "nice person," not living a life.

Being nice and having your needs met are not in conflict. In fact, when your life is fulfilling, life is easier and more joyful. I'm not sure if we can ever be 100 percent fulfilled; but the closer you get, the happier you will be. Being nice becomes an extension of who you are, not a role you play to please others.

It's exhausting to try to take care of everyone around you. As time goes by, you move farther from the authentic you. When you agree to something or tolerate something or someone in your life that is causing you stress, you create an internal conflict. Like air slowly leaking from a tire, the quality of your life will drain away.

It's difficult to be generous if your self-doubt has prevented you from seeking a raise or a higher-paying position or from starting your own business. You will never be happy in a relationship where you are meeting the needs of the other person, yet having none of your needs met.

One of the first steps toward getting your needs met is to learn to recognize word and thought patterns that currently control and manipulate you.

LIBERATING YOURSELF FROM "SHOULD"

In my opinion, the one word that has created walls of massive self-doubt and controlling, manipulative guilt is the word "should." In the family of "should" are "ought to," "must," "have to," and other words and phrases that presuppose rules and standards. They imply a consequence or guilt if they are not adhered to.

"Should" is at the root of all guilt. Much of your negative programming is a result of the word "should" being attached to some action. "You should clean your plate." "You should not ask for money." "You should think more about others." When someone "shoulds on you," they are imposing their rules of life and behavior upon you. When you should on someone else, you are imposing your rules of life and how to act upon them. Should creates stress for the should-er and the should-ee.

The more your world is a world of shoulds, the more stressed you are because everyone has his own set of rules. The world is not going to follow your rules, so relax and just take care of yourself. You are the only person you can control. Shoulds try to control others, which is impossible.

In some cultures, parents build a world within tight, often counterproductive rules of, "You should do this," "You shouldn't do that." The result of thousands of shoulds throughout a childhood is an irrational view of the world. Why? Because one person's shouldn't is another person's should.

Certainly, we need laws and rules in life. There are also extreme behaviors that most people would agree are unacceptable. Random killing, rape, child abuse, etc. But the day-to-day activities you experience will be much easier to deal with if you can liberate yourself from shoulding on yourself and others.

The next time a car races past you, it might be more helpful to think of why he may be driving so fast, rather than say or think, "He shouldn't be driving so fast." He could be late for work. He could be trying to get his pregnant wife or sick child to the hospital. His family may be in an accident. When my family was in the accident, I ran red lights and drove on sidewalks, trying to get to them.

Learn to reframe "should" into "That's interesting. I wish he wouldn't do that, but I have no control over it." Another strategy is to replace "should" with "could." "Could" offers possibilities that "should" shuts out.

LIVING IN ABSOLUTES

To me, "should" is an absolute. Absolutes are words that trap you and the person you are talking to into a black-and-white scenario when the truth is that reality is multihued.

Other absolutes include "can't," "won't," "never," "always," and "everyone." Absolutes cut off opportunity and possibility. Absolutes are usually negative exaggerations. Children insist, "Mom! Everyone is wearing this. I have to have one!" The parent recognizes the absurdity of the notion that everyone is wearing the same product and that her daughter does not have to have one.

However, does that same adult catch herself saying, "We can't afford that . . ." or "That will never work . . ." Or "I can't do anything right . . ." or "I always overeat . . ."? These are all negative absolutes that bind you by cutting off any other possibilities. Absolutes are the easy way out. Not only do these word patterns not require any creativity, they eliminate it.

Learn to replace absolute words and phrases with those that give you a chance. For instance, author Robert T. Kiyosaki in his excellent book, *Rich Dad, Poor Dad*, suggest that the common thought pattern of "We can't afford that . . ." be changed to "How can we afford that?" This kind of thinking pushes you to explore ways you could afford it. You may very well end up deciding not to make the purchase, but developing this habit of thinking beyond the can'ts and absolutes will expand your horizons considerably.

When you adapt this mind-set—and believe me, it takes practice—you become curious about the lessons life offers rather than feeling stress about events and people you can't control. You begin to see opportunities and possibilities that have always existed, but your "shoulds" and your "absolutes" worked like blinders on a horse to keep you from seeing what was around you all the time.

LEARN TO SAY "THANK YOU"

A classic impostor syndrome symptom is the discounting or denial of praise. How hard is saying thank you? It may be harder than you think. Whether you can simply say "thank you" for a compliment is a telltale measure of your self-doubt or self-confidence.

Many of us got mixed messages growing up about the importance of being humble. If we accept praise, we fear that other people will think we are bragging. For some people, accepting praise means that they agree with the compliment. This is difficult when you have a lingering guilt about success. Also, this is compounded in the impostor syndrome when we really don't want to draw attention to ourselves for fear we'll be discovered as, well, impostors.

For years, as I was coming up the ranks as a martial artist, I got compliments on my technique or a form. I always begged off and said something like, "Ah. I should have pivoted more on the sidekick . . ." My self-doubt would not allow me to accept a compliment. It wasn't until I was in my early thirties that I began to realize that I never failed to deflect or defray a compliment. It was as though I apologized for the attention.

When you simply respond to a compliment with a sincere and unapologetic "thank you," you drive home to your subconscious a message that you are worthy of praise. You feed your self-esteem the idea that you do certain things well. This is not as easy as it may seem, but it's true and it works.

Learn to Say "No"

Recognizing that we are all lazy by nature (see "Setting New Strategies"), it's natural that if someone can get you to do something for them rather than do it themselves, they will. How often do you take on time-consuming, stress-creating tasks for others that they could either do themselves or outsource? Many of us have been conditioned that we are selfish if we say no to a request for help. Certainly, if someone is in serious danger or need, there are ways we can help. But because of the lazy nature of humans, people will seek out people who find it difficult to say no and will transfer their tasks, problems, and projects to them.

Learning to say no is an important step in destroying your self-doubt. The next time someone asks you to do something that you don't want to do or that will not move you closer to your goals, simply say no.

Of course, there are times when you are faced with a request for help from a boss or supervisor who will not respond well to a rebuke from you. Instead of saying no to your boss, try this, "Okay. Help me understand what you are asking me to do, and then you can help me decide what the priorities are. Right now I'm working on this, this, and this. They are important because of this reason. What would you like me NOT to do, in order to do this?" This is a good way of communicating that you are hard at work and have a full plate but that you are willing to help out if the new task has priority over the current workload.

In this scenario, you're not saying no but instead are leading your boss to the conclusion that she may not want to give you the project because you are doing more important work. This again is the classic martial arts principle of align and redirect.

You align with your boss and redirect her to take the work elsewhere. Best of all, you make it seem like it's her decision.

Taking Care of Your Body

All we can control is what we do and how we think. The one area of your life that you have the most control over is what you put in your mouth and how you keep active and moving.

Healthy people make eating smart and exercising a priority. Unhealthy people make other activities a priority. It's always interesting to me when a client says they don't have time to exercise, yet they spend an hour or two each day watching TV or surfing the net. We all have the same twenty-four hours each day. We just don't have the same priorities.

When I was teaching my karate classes each night, I would remind the students that while they were with me, sweating and pushing themselves, the rest of the world was at home watching TV and eating ice cream. I wanted them to associate pain with watching TV and pleasure with training and growing.

Watching TV, playing video games, surfing the net are all mind-numbing experiences. They put you in a trance that helps you forget the stresses of the day. The problem is that they have no long-term benefits. That is short-term gain for long-term pain. Ten years of those activities result in a steady deterioration of your health and happiness.

I don't think there is a better example of short-term pain for long-term gain than eating smart and exercising. Taking twenty minutes to exercise is a great way to eliminate stress and improve the quality of your life. If twenty minutes is too much right now, make it five minutes or one minute, for that matter. The point is to make your body move.

Think one minute is not long enough? Try doing squats for a full minute. Try doing push-ups for a full minute. You will find out quickly that you can get a great workout in just sixty seconds. In fact, visit my Web site, www.OneMinuteWorkout.com, for some direction on how to get the best results in the shortest period of time.

Healthy people make it a priority of their day to take care of their bodies first. When they shop, they read labels and choose healthy food. When they go out, they read the menu, looking for the healthiest dinners first and then choosing from that group only. Most menus are designed for overeaters. Next time you go to a restaurant, look at what people are eating and what shape they are in. You'll see fat people eating fried, fatty food while healthier people are eating chicken, fish, salads, or lean beef. There is a reason fat people are fat. They don't take care of themselves first. You are 100 percent responsible for what you put into your mouth.

The list of strategies for taking care of yourself first is much longer than this chapter. In many ways, this entire book is designed to help you to get more of your needs met so that you in turn can help others. This is an important mind-set, and it's one that is like walking up the down escalator. You have to keep at it, or you will start going backward before you know it.

Getting Your Needs Met Exercise

The process of learning to take care of your needs first starts with self-assessment. Over the next week, make a note of

1. Every time you agree to something you would have preferred to say "No" to.
2. Every time you receive a compliment and how you respond.
3. Every time you hear someone receive a compliment and how he or she responds to it.
4. Every time you use the word "should." See if you can reframe the "should" into something more reasonable.
5. Every time someone else uses "should" on you or someone else.
6. Every time you could take better care of yourself but don't. Track the times you prioritize TV, net surfing, or any other sedentary, mind-numbing activities over exercise.
7. Every time you do something for someone else that you would like to have done for yourself but didn't.

Chapter Twenty

CREATING A FUTURE THAT IS GREATER THAN YOUR PAST

Looking back on the present.

Having children was a huge step toward helping me ponder my own mortality. I often think of how far along the spectrum of my life span I am at any given time. My goal is always to create a future that is greater than my past.

Here is an interesting exercise that I learned from attending Dan Sullivan's Strategic Coach Program. This is designed to help you gain a perspective on the time line of your life.

1. How long do you think you will live?

I turned forty-five when I did this exercise; and for some reason, that strikes me as about the halfway point for my life; so the number that comes to mind for me is ninety years of age. What's yours?_____

2. How would you like to describe yourself at that age?

Here are some of the ways I hope will accurately describe me in the final years of my life.

Physical—Still training, good diet, strong, flexible

Mental—Wise, patient, intuitive, sharp, still writing, still teaching, future-focused mind (not frozen in the past)

Financial—Independent (don't have to work for money), six-figure passive income

Relationships—Loving and intimate with my wife, loving and close to my children, still teaching

3. With modern science, the odds of your living longer are good and getting better. If you are able to add twenty years to the number above, what would you do with that time?*

Here are some of my answers:

a. Continue to teach and mentor young people about entrepreneurship and the attitudes of success
b. Spend that much more time with my family
c. Continue to learn every day

WHAT WOULD YOU DO WITH THE EXTRA YEARS?

Of course, the real purpose of this is to backtrack to today to determine what kind of life you need to live now to lead to your description above. Clearly, if you plan to be financially independent at that time, you can't start saving the year before. If you want to be healthy, it has to start now. Most important of all, how would you like to look back on your relationships when there is no time left to change them?

This kind of exercise is stimulating and also sobering. The perspective of being at the end and looking back can help you look at each day with longer and wiser perspective. It certainly does for me.

Chapter Twenty-One

YOU ARE THE MOVE YOU MAKE

You've got to want to succeed.

The title of this chapter is borrowed from my favorite band, Yes. The lead singer and driving force behind the band, Jon Anderson, in his own unique style, has always written songs about hope and believing in yourself. Through the years, I've drawn tremendous inspiration from his work. This title sums up one of the most powerful lessons I've learned. Simply put, you are responsible for your success. No one else is. Not your parents, your community, your government, or your friends. It's all up to you. While that may seem harsh, if you reframe it a little, it's liberating. You are the move you make.

While it's nearly impossible to succeed without the help of others, once you embrace the idea that you are the driving force behind your own situation, you realize the only person holding you back is you.

The life you live right now is the life you have created for yourself so far. If this life is not what you want, you have to start making the decisions and taking the actions necessary to create the life you desire.

As we have explored together, it's critical that you realize that the past doesn't define you. What has happened has happened. If you got fired, dumped, divorced, bankrupted, injured, sick, or born into a family of wackos, guess what? There are countless stories of people overcoming those same circumstances to create wonderful lives.

Look at the past as your school. This school has taught you some important lessons that you can take into the future. The key is to look back on the past without emotion. This is not always easy to do, but imagine you are kind of an experience auditor peeking into the past of a client. Your job is to analyze objectively what happened and why it happened and to extract the most positive lesson possible from the experience.

Maybe, because of self-doubt, you allowed a situation to worsen until something bad happened. Maybe you let a relationship go on for way too long; or you put off making an important business call, and you lost the account. What happened can't be changed, but recognizing and taking responsibility for not letting that self-doubt control you again will fortify you as you move forward in creating your new future.

LOTS OF EXCUSES, BUT NO GOOD REASONS

If you are unhappy in your current state of life, you can come up with all kinds of excuses, but not one good reason for not creating the life you want. This was a huge realization for me.

As I said, my parents spent much of their time under extreme financial tension. Like most people, they were never taught how to manage money; so when they had it, they spent it until they were out of control and deeply in debt.

Since happiness is a direct result of the level of control you have in your life, you can imagine the level of unhappiness in a household that is in perpetual financial turmoil.

My parents loved me and worked very hard to provide for my sister, brothers, and me. They were simply raised in a way that was typical of the post-Depression era. Money was never discussed except to lament how little they had.

Work was described to me by my dad as something everyone "hates," and there was never any discussion of the possibilities the world offered. The attitude was that you could not control your destiny beyond deciding if you wanted to drive a truck or wait on tables.

Success seemed to be reserved for people on television, who all seemed like the heartless banker from *It's a Wonderful Life*. The rich were people who had sold their souls for money and would throw you out on the street to keep it.

This would probably be a more predictable story if I said that I was inspired by my parents' despair and resolved never to be in that situation. That's partially true. Because money was such an issue, I developed a kind of a "hippie" attitude that money was not important and the desire for material possessions was bourgeoisie. In a nutshell, I was clueless about money as well.

Remember, this was the early and mid-1970s. I bought into the idea that I was not going to be rich, but I did not agree to being miserable at my job. My martial arts training provided me with a great outlet for my self-growth. I resolved to teach martial arts for a living. Still, I had no fantasies of growing rich as a result of my teaching.

I just loved to teach and train; and as a martial artist, I was accorded a level of respect and inclusion that was very satisfying to an eighteen-year-old. Since I had been programmed to believe that financial success was out of my control, I chose instead to control at least how I spent my day. I figured that if I were not going to make any money, I might as well enjoy myself. I chose quality of life over financial possibility, which, as you know now, is short-term gain for long-term pain.

Since classes were at night, I slept as late as I wanted each morning and then trained all day before wandering in to the karate school at about 5 p.m. to teach. It was like being a surf bum in a gi (karate uniform). I was indeed a karate jock; and it was fun, for a while.

Mentored by a Millionaire

It was not until I opened my school—almost a decade later—that I started to envision that I could be successful. At that time, I began to give private lessons to a doctor, Richard Phares, whom I mentioned earlier. Dr. Phares had already been a millionaire for over fifteen years by then. He was an eccentric fellow and loved to sit and talk with me about his views on the world, which included the process of wealth building.

No one had ever discussed these subjects with me before. At the time, I was riding my ten-speed bike to my karate school because I could not afford a car. He was driving a big gold Mercedes Benz. I had never been in a car this expensive. That was when my thinking started to change, and my vision of the future began to expand.

Dr. Phares exposed me to a lifestyle of wealth and opulence that I had never dreamed of. At the time, I was getting a lot of local press attention because of my success with the U.S. kickboxing team in Europe, and I had a TV show; so I was pretty high profile. I was the local karate star. Though I had no money, I was an accomplished athlete who was seen on television every week. I guess that made up for my lack of net worth. Dr. Phares seemed to enjoy introducing me to his associates as his personal instructor, the "world-champion black belt."

We met with his wealthy friends and went to his million-dollar home for barbecues with his family. They seemed like normal people to me, not heartless, money-hoarding villains. They donated to charities and volunteered in the community. The main difference was that they openly discussed business and business strategies.

This exposure began to reprogram my thinking with regard to money and what my potential really was. Until that point, I never thought of such a life because I had never seen it or experienced it. It is hard to create a taste for something you have never seen or felt.

It was also about this time that I began listening to what must be by now thousands of audio programs on personal and professional success. Learning methods of business and how to succeed through these audio programs, while expanding my perspective through Dr. Phares's world, accelerated my reprogramming and created a strong desire to grow as a person, a teacher, and a businessman.

I tell you this because it was so powerful for me that I can only hope it is as powerful for you. In order to change your outer world, you must change your inner world. I had to change my programming and references in order to begin the process of changing my reality.

By immersing myself in study and seeking out people who had been there already, I began to destroy my self-doubt. I learned how to speak, to sell, to have a conversation, to negotiate, and to succeed.

I began to realize that I was 100 percent responsible for reaching the level of success I desired. I realized that even though Dr. Phares could show me how the rich live and Brian Tracy could teach me how to get there, only I could make it happen. "If it's to be, it's up to me" became my mantra.

PROSPERITY CONSCIOUSNESS

I started to develop a "prosperity consciousness." This is a mind-set, or heightened awareness, of the great possibilities the world presents. In this realm, the world became a huge menu of opportunities. The opportunities had always been there, but I couldn't see them before. My programming while growing up led me to "poverty consciousness"—the mind-set that you will always struggle for money and privilege. "We can't afford that" was the mantra of my parents.

I knew it would be a long, tough road and that no one was going to do it for me. As daunting a task as that was, I also began to realize that, for the first time, I was talking to myself as though it could actually happen. To think that I could actually burst out of the chains of mediocrity and become a success was so radical a thought that it shot right through me.

Once I allowed myself to believe that I could be a success and then followed that with the conscious decision to go for it, my life changed. My outer world began to evolve into a world of opportunities that I had not seen before. It was as though I had been seeing a black-and-white world, and suddenly the color was switched on. This is the power of making the decision to be a success and then taking full responsibility for achieving it.

The very important truth you must face is that only you can control you. You cannot control the economy or other people or how you were raised. You can only control you. If you do not like what you see in the mirror, you cannot break the mirror to change what you see. You have to change what the mirror reflects. You have to change from the inside out. This is an important realization in transforming your beliefs, which is a critical step in reducing and then eliminating self-doubt.

This is also why in the first year of my martial arts students' training, my emphasis in their training is 90 percent mental and 10 percent physical. I have to first get them to believe they can earn a black belt just like I want you to believe you can accomplish your goals and dreams.

It's difficult to improve anything 100 percent overnight. However, if you set a goal of 1 or 2 percent improvement per week, you'll have a 50 to 100 percent improvement in a year. You can make it happen, and I know you will. You deserve to succeed and achieve your goals as much as I do. Just like my friend told me all those many years ago, "I know you, and you would not accept anything less."

RESPONSIBILITY EXERCISE

1. If everyone in your family were just like you, what kind of family would it be?

2. If everyone at work were just like you, what kind of work environment would it be?

3. Where in your life have you been blaming someone or something else for your situation?

4. Name some positive people you could associate with who would expand your perspective on life and your future.

Dear Reader,

Congratulations! Reading this book is a great step towards overcoming self-doubt and taking control of your life. You, like me, enjoy personal growth and associating with like-minded, success oriented people who will support you in your path.

What I've found is that readers like you enjoy continuing to learn by taking advantage of my live mentoring programs and seminars. Following the principles in this book and additional strategies I've learned and developed, our programs will help you or your organization to:

1. **Rediscover Youthful Energy and Improve Your Health:** Without good health, nothing matters. Our program is designed to help you rediscover your youthful energy and curiosity about life.

2. **Gain Financial Independence:** Freedom and security in our world is purchased with dollars. Imagine your life where you never have to worry about money again and you have a six figure cushion to land on.

3. **Become a Powerful, and Persuasive Communicator:** Your ability to succeed in life is in direct proportion to your ability to communicate and persuade others to assist you in your quest for success.

4. **Learn the Secret to Unshakable Self-Confidence:** Nothing holds smart, talented people back more than self-doubt. Our program is specially designed to help you overcome self-doubt and build self-confidence.

5. **Increase Your Level of Attraction:** Attraction is the key to a fruitful life. This is attracting the people, events, and abundance into your life that will help you achieve your dreams.

6. **Peer-to-Peer Accountability:** This is a key advantage of the John Graden Accelerated Success Program. Many students have said this was the single most powerful motivator for them to take action.

7. **Peer-to-Peer Support Network:** Each of us will encounter challenges along the way. That is part of the journey. However, you will be supported by me as your mentor and your peer group. Many close, profitable, and meaningful relationships have been born out of these classes.

As a reader of The Impostor Syndrome, you are eligible for a 10% discount off of any of our products or programs. Please visit www.JohnGraden.com to review our latest catalog.

Whether you personally would like to continue your work with me or you would like to bring me in to work with your organization, I stand ready to serve you and look forward to getting to know you as we move forward together.

Thanks again for allowing me into your life.

Your friend,

John Graden
www.JohnGraden.com

Get Published, Inc!
Thorofare, NJ 08086
24 August 2009
BA2009236